Dictionary of
Heraldry

BROCKHAMPTON PRESS
LONDON

This edition published 1997 by Brockhampton Press, a member of the
Hodder Headline PLC Group

ISBN 1 86019 711 6

Printed and bound in the UK

19396

CONTENTS

INTRODUCTION

Heraldry is a fascinating subject that probably has its origins in medieval times but is also connected by certain elements to even more distant history. That these links are tenuous is almost inevitable, but much depends upon the precise definition of the term. For most purposes, and according to the majority of students of the subject, heraldry today is the science of armory, i.e. the rules and guidelines that regulate the use and interpretation of the diverse pictures, emblems and other elements that relate to a shield, helmet or the achievement in total. Armory therefore does not include additional topics such as lines of descent (pedigree) or ceremonial practice, but these do fall within the scope of heraldry. In the main, this book will deal with the various elements of armory, describing their variety, the terminology and providing appropriate interpretations.

Medieval history spans many centuries, and to say armory has its origins in this era is hardly precise. To be a little more specific, it seems that armory can be traced back to the time of the Crusades, which in themselves spanned almost two centuries. Some authors quote examples of heraldry from many years BC, but none, understandably, is related to a shield of any description, hence they cannot be said to be a part of armory. Also, a variety of figures that feature in heraldry can be seen from centuries past, but they do not occur in heraldic form and were used in other ways.

There are references to the hereditary decoration of weapons in the Third Crusade (1189–92), and when shields were first used they were painted, although not necessarily for the purposes of identification in battle. Various ornaments were applied to shield and helmet before the appearance of the closed helmet. This was supposedly the reason why armory came to the fore—to aid in the identification of an individual when the facial features were covered. Weapons were obviously very important to a soldier, and whenever possible a sword and shield would pass to a son, thus establishing a link between armory and family (i.e. heredity), with the ornament of the shield being retained in the line. In the early 1200s, the closed helmet was introduced, thus hiding the wearer's face and necessitating a means of identification. Thus the decorations on his shield and the ornaments on his helmet and his surcoat would all serve to identify the individual. Eventually the system developed to the point where an individual displayed symbols on his shield, etc, that allowed not only identifying marks to be seen but his family history to be revealed. By the middle of the 13th century, heraldry could be identified as a distinctive field of study.

AUTHORITIES IN HERALDRY

The word 'herald' has its origins in Middle English via Old French, which itself was derived from the Germanic. Control and regulation of coat armour was devolved from the Crown to heralds and officers of arms. It seems the function of the herald began, perhaps around the beginning of the 13th century, in the guise of a steward who looked after the running of festivities. Many were also minstrels, who would recount the events of a battle or tournament after the event. This was then applied to individuals, at least those of sufficient power and standing who would have their own herald to tell of his, and his ancestors', undertakings. The herald wore the coat of arms of his master and, in effect, was a messenger who was not involved in fighting. As tournaments became popular, the herald also took on the task of checking the arms of those participating, thus acquiring knowledge of coat armour. In due course, royal heralds gained an understanding of the arms of the principal families and, through them, the sovereign acquired control over these arms.

The official right to grant arms was given to the heralds by Edward III, but one formal body was not created until 1483 in the reign of Richard III, about one hundred years later. However, the role of the herald was clearly set out early in the 15th century when William Bruges was made Garter King of Arms by King Henry V.

The headquarters of heraldry in England is the College of Arms and the hereditary head is the Earl Marshal. This role developed from when the Earl Marshal (or just plain Marshal) was, with the Lord High Constable, the first in rank militarily beneath the sovereign. A variety of duties thus fell to the Marshal, including the disposition of troops and associated bodies. This was achieved by use of a variety of crests, banners, standards, and such like, so that Marshals became well versed in their study, and ultimately this knowledge was recorded, affording them a somewhat elevated position. They then became involved in negotiations on battlefields, declarations of war or peace and the arrangement of less belligerent ceremonial occasions, including coronations.

Under the Earl Marshal there are three kings of arms, then six heralds of arms (in England) and four pursuivants of arms. The three kings of arms are Garter (the principal king of arms), who heads the College of Arms; Clarenceux, who deals with matters of heraldry in south, east and west England south of the River Trent; and Norroy, who functions similarly north of the Trent.

In Scotland, the Lord Lyon King of Arms occupies a similar role to that of the Earl Marshal. The office of Lord Lyon can be traced back to the 15th century, but the title was officially recognized in Parliament in 1663 and ratified by the Scottish Parliament in 1672. There are three heralds and three pursuivants beneath the Lord Lyon. Rothesay, Albany and Marchmont are the heralds, Unicorn, Ormond and Carrick the pursuivants. The Court of the Lord Lyon is now situated in HM New Register House in Edinburgh.

The Lord Lyon King of Arms is not answerable to the Earl Marshal but occupies a highly responsible position overseeing several functions that in England are dealt with by the Earl Marshal and other departments. The Lord Lyon is involved with all ceremonial aspects of state, royal and public occasions, and he is also a judge of the realm. Heraldic business in Scotland is managed through the Court of the Lord Lyon, where judicial procedures are followed, but most applications do not require legal assistance. The earliest known examples of Scottish armory are found on the seals of Allan, High Stewart of Scotland, and Patrick, Earl of Dunbar. These are dated at around 1177 and 1182 respectively.

Heraldry had at the outset the practical use of identification and was adopted by clan chiefs, landowners, high figures in the church, eminent soldiers, etc. As such, the science became associated with nobility or high rank. Scotland is well known for its clan system, and because there is a relatively small number of families or clans, the heraldic system has developed along quite different lines compared to most other countries. Individual clans may have many members, and a significant proportion may lay claim to being of noble lineage. This has resulted in a fairly small number of coats of arms but there are many variations on the basic theme.

The first signs of such authority in Ireland appears around the mid-16th century with the appointment of the first Ulster king of arms by Edward VI in 1552. Whereas in England the king of arms makes a grant of arms under the authority of the Earl Marshal, for Irish grants the Ulster king of arms complies with and grants the application. From the late 16th to the end of the 17th century, funeral certificates were used in Ireland, and officers of arms attended the appropriate ceremonies, i.e. the funerals of individuals who carried arms. In general there was a paucity of records in Ireland, and the funeral certificates gave evidence of the right to bear arms. The growing difficulty in proving lines of descent in Ireland was dealt with by confirming through letters patent arms that had been borne by three generations over at least one hundred years. The current situation is that Northern Ireland is handled by the Norroy King of Arms (who is thus titled Norroy and Ulster King of Arms) who also has the right to confirm arms if the 'hundred-year rule' can be met.

In Ireland the office of the Chief Herald and the State Heraldic Museum are housed in the Genealogical Office in Dublin.

BEARING ARMS

The right to bear arms is therefore dependent upon receipt of authority from the necessary body. This may be through a *grant of arms*, a *confirmation of arms* (in Ireland) or a recording or confirmation at what was called a *visitation*.

Visitations began in the early 16th century and involved heralds travelling around the country to check on all claims to arms. If they were happy with what they saw, then it was registered or confirmed. These occurrences ceased in the late 1680s, but the reports are preserved in the College of Arms. A confirmation thus gave full rights to bear the arms but succeeding members of the family had to prove their line of descent. However, when a grant is now made, it is given to the applicant and his descendants but future generations must register at the office of arms to build up the line of descent.

THE ACHIEVEMENT

'Coat of arms' is a loose term that encompasses the whole of the armorial device. Technically, in the science of heraldry, this is called the *achievement*. Coat of arms has its origin in the tabard or surcoat worn over armour by knights. This over-garment had embroidered on it a copy of the design to be found on the shield. Everyone who is authorized to bear arms will have an achievement, which comprises the shield and certain accessories, all of which relate to medieval military items. In addition to the shield, there is a helmet, with mantling, wreath, crest and motto. Further, and especially in the case of persons of higher rank, there may be supporters, a coronet of rank, a badge and additional insignia. All these various elements are set out in a particular way, and there follows a description of each, in some cases there being numerous variations on the main theme.

The *shield* is the central and most important part of the achievement. The rules of armory are concerned primarily with the shield, and all the other elements are contingent upon it. In heraldry it is called the *escutcheon*, and it bears the arms, the signs and depictions of the appropriate name. The figures on a shield are called *charges*. Much of heraldry comprises the selection and placing of charges, and the arrangement of the charges on the shield is termed their *marshalling*.

The shield can be of any shape, and it has varied in the past depending on fashion, as there are no rules to be followed. The shield or shape upon which the arms were depicted could thus be circular, square, oval, a banner or similar shape. Just because an armorial design is not shown on a shield does not mean it is not a coat of arms. The one exception is that the lozenge shape is used for women. Apart from female Scottish chiefs, women may not use crests or helmets, and, by implication, wreath and mantling, and their arms therefore appear on a lozenge shape. The role of women in Scotland was different from that in England, Scottish ladies being much more independent, and in medieval times both husband and wife held much the same station when it came to matters of armory. They could each bear their own arms (the father's in the case of a woman), and the wife could use supporters or coronet where appropriate. This was very different from the situation in England where, in effect, a married woman had no individuality or identity.

Heraldry is strewn with terminology, some of it convoluted, and a number of terms associated with the shield provide a good example. Marshalling has already been mentioned; painting or drawing the charges on a shield is called *emblazoning*, and the task of describing the resulting arrangement is *blazoning*.

In an achievement, the *helmet* is placed on top of the shield unless it belongs to a peer, in which case his coronet is placed between the top of the shield and the helmet. As with shields, the shapes and styles vary and indicate a particular rank, but inevitably over the years the designs have acquired embellishments and styles quite inappropriate to the function of a helmet. On the top of the helmet would be found the *crest*. This developed from the ridge running over the apex of the helmet (which was a protective device, should a blow be received to the head) and the plume. Crests were originally limited to those of higher rank but now can be granted to all, save a few exceptions (including the clergy).

The *wreath* (otherwise known as the *torse*) is a circular configuration of two strands twisted together, somewhat resembling a rope. It comprises two colours (although in heraldry, 'colour' has a particular significance, *see* page 20) that match those of the mantling (*see* below). The wreath is placed around the dome of the helmet and the base of the crest.

The *mantling* (or *lambrequin*) is the veil-like cloth that is draped from the top of the helmet and down either side of the shield. This derives from the cloth worn by knights to lessen the effect of the sun. This would have been a particular problem in the Crusades, when the burning sun would have caused considerable problems to anyone wearing armour. This manner of protection would hardly have been necessary in cooler climes, but a further benefit was that the material would help deaden the cut of a blade, and it could be that a sword might become entangled in the mantling. Inevitably, this would have led to the material becoming torn and ragged, and it seems artists took this as an opportunity to represent the mantling with various embellishments. Indeed, heraldic artists through the ages seem to have assumed a certain artistic licence in this, and all sorts of mantlings may be seen.

If a *motto* appears as part of the achievement, it commonly appears on a scroll. It is usually positioned beneath the achievement, but in Scotland it is often placed above the crest. There is also a difference in the regulations between Scotland and England. In Scotland, the motto forms part of the achievement that is registered while in England it is not included in the grant of arms. In many cases the motto has been or has evolved from a war cry.

In addition to these major items in an achievement, there may be other elements, such as coronets, insignia, chapeaux and, in particular, supporters. *Heraldic supporters* are figures placed to either side of the shield and may be human, beasts (especially the lion, but a diverse array of animals is seen), monsters (mythical and legendary creatures such as the gryphon, unicorn and dragon) and birds. A whole host of animals in addition to these can be found in achievements, but usually as charges rather than supporters. In the main, supporters appear on the arms of individuals of high rank, such as members of royalty, peers, knights, and so on.

The following sections describe the components of the achievement more fully and the importance of position, colour and other factors.

USE OF COLOUR IN HERALDRY

The surface of the shield in heraldry is called the *field*, and the field or its divisions are *tinctured*, i.e. they are coloured. Tinctures are divided into *colours*, *metals* and also *furs*. In essence, therefore, the field is the colour of the background, or ground of the shield, when there is just one colour. If there are two or more colours or tinctures, then these comprise the field.

There are two metals, gold and silver, and as with other tinctures, each has a technical abbreviation. Gold is therefore called *or* and silver *argent*, which is shortened to *arg.* (and the full stop is included). In most cases, yellow and white will be substituted for or and arg. in emblazonments, although thin gold or silver leaf may be used if expense is no object. When describing an achievement, the adjectival part always follows the noun, so a golden lion is termed 'a lion or'. This is because of the origin of heraldic terminology, which can be traced back to the Norman French in which this structure was used. If more than one adjective is used to qualify a noun, then the one relating to the tincture comes last, thus one would see 'a lion rampant, or'. Yellow has been used greatly in emblazonments and always represents gold. The usage of silver or a representative alternative is less common than gold. This may in part be because of the difficulty of preserving the colour. Any parts intended to be arg. are therefore left blank on a white background material or painted white. In a monochrome representation, arg. is therefore blank while or is depicted by small dots.

In addition to the two metals, there are five colours: red, black, blue, green and purple. These are termed and abbreviated as:

red is known as *gules* and its abbreviation is *gu*.
black is known as *sable* and its abbreviation is *sa*.
blue is known as *azure* and its abbreviation is *az*.
purple is known as *purpure* and its abbreviation is *purp*.
green is known as *vert* and is not abbreviated.

On monochrome, i.e. uncoloured, representations, these colours are represented by particular ornaments, shadings or hatchings (figure 1). This system was developed a long time ago when the real colours could not be used. The first attempts were made in the 17th century, and that of Petia Sancta (1638) has stood the test of time. Some authors, particularly on the Continent, developed additional hatchings to represent other colours (figure 2). English heraldry makes mention of two colours in addition to

Figure 1: The major hatchings used in heraldry

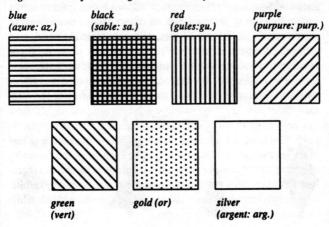

blue *(azure: az.)*	*black* *(sable: sa.)*	*red* *(gules:gu.)*	*purple* *(purpure: purp.)*

green *(vert)*	*gold (or)*	*silver* *(argent: arg.)*

Figure 2: Other colour hatchings

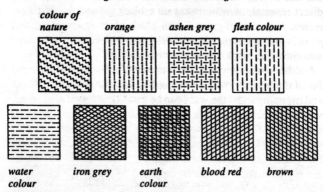

colour of
nature   orange   ashen grey   flesh colour

water   iron grey   earth   blood red   brown
colour   colour

the five, but they are used very rarely. These are *tenné*, which is represented by horizontal and diagonal lines together (diagonally as in purpure) and is a yellow brown, and *sanguine* or *murrey*, which combines the diagonal lines of both vert and purpure and which, as might be expected, is a blood shade of red.

Although the system of hatching exists, most records tend to be in colour and this applies particularly to official records.

The third type of tincture is the *furs*. Initially, there were just two furs, called *ermine* and *vair*. Ermine is white with black spots that represent the tails of the animal and there are a number of different spot types to be found (*see* figure 3). There

Figure 3: Some types of ermine spots

are also several variations of ermine with differing colours. A direct reversal, of white spots on a black ground, is called *ermines*. A gold background with black spots is *erminois*, and *pean* is gold spots on a black background. Occasionally ermine was shown as black spots on a silver field.

Another commonly used fur was *vair*. This is derived from the fur of the squirrel, which was used widely for medieval linings and trimmings, and the word can be traced from the Latin *varus*, via Old French and Middle English derivations. We are told that the story of Cinderella came from the French and her slippers were made of fur. In the translation, 'vair' being similar to *verre* for 'glass', the slippers were transformed into glass. The heraldic representation of vair is supposed to match the blue-grey back and white front of the animal. Thus, when joined together the effect is of rows of alternating blue and white cup shapes. This sinuous line has undergone change over the years, and the result is a fixed geometrical arrangement of shapes in which a reversed shape exactly matches those on either side, which are not reversed (figure 4). It seems that there is no rule as to how many rows of vair should be used.

Divisions of the field similar to vair are found. Although vair is always blue and white, other colours are used in variation. These are called *vairy* and can employ any two tinctures (usually a colour and a metal). *Contrevair* or *countervair* is an ar-

Figure 4: Vair

Figure 5: Contrevair

Figure 6: Vair in pale

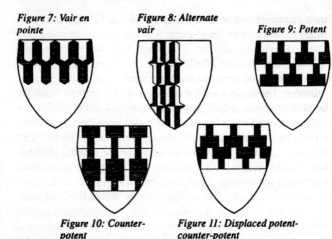

Figure 7: Vair en pointe

Figure 8: Alternate vair

Figure 9: Potent

Figure 10: Counter-potent

Figure 11: Displaced potent-counter-potent

rangement whereby the points and bases of the shapes of one row meet those of the rows above and below (figure 5). *Vair in pale* is where the columns are arranged such that shapes of a like colour all fall vertically beneath each other (figure 6). In addition to these, further categories are *vair en pointe*, in which the shapes have their apices pointing in the same direction column by column but are alternately reversed and not reversed (figure 7), and *alternate vair*, in which the shapes are bisected vertically, as shown in figure 8. Vair is borne by quite an appreciable number of families in Britain and Europe.

Two further furs are sometimes seen, *potent* and the less common form, *counter-potent* (figures 9 and 10). It is not difficult to recognize the similarity between potent and vair, and the former may well have evolved from the latter by virtue of 'artistic licence'. In some accounts, potent is called *potent-counter-potent*, which, for obvious reasons, is better simplified to potent. Even more complex names and styles can be found, such as the German *displaced potent-counter-potent* (figure 11), but this is not likely to be met very frequently.

RULE GOVERNING TINCTURES

In the placing of tinctures there are certain rules that must be followed. The fundamental stipulation is that a colour must not be placed upon a colour, nor a metal upon a metal, thus if the field or shield surface is a colour, it may receive only a metal or a fur. The converse applies if the field is a metal—it can take only a colour or a fur. Furs may be placed on metal or colour, and indeed it is permitted to place one fur on another but it is not a common occurrence. There are certain exceptions to this rule, notably for charges 'proper', divided fields, and the edges of animals, e.g. the claws of a lion. A *charge proper* (abbreviated where necessary to *ppr.*) is when a charge is shown in its natural colours, so a tree would be essentially brown for the trunk and branches, and green for the leaves.

The rule regarding superimposition of tinctures is helpful in determining the marshalling of charges on a shield and in eluci-dating their relative positions. If a charge coloured black had edges of red on a shield, it would have to be one charge edged, or *fimbriated*, with another colour because the rules would not permit a red charge on top of a black charge.

THE SHIELD

As already mentioned, the background of the shield is called a *field*, and objects placed upon it are called *charges*.

DIVISIONS OF THE FIELD

There are several terms used to describe and classify the field and its subdivision. The side of the shield on the left when viewed from the front is the *dexter* side, and the right side of the shield when viewed in the same way is called the *sinister* side.

This is clearly because, when borne by someone, the dexter side of the shield is, as expected, to the right; similarly with the sinister and left side. In addition, there are specific points in the field that are used to describe the position of charges and any lines dividing the field (figure 12). These are:

1 dexter chief point
2 middle chief point
3 sinister chief point
4 honour point
5 fess or centre point
6 nombrill point or navel
7 dexter base point
8 middle base point
9 sinister base point

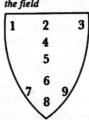

Figure 12: Points on the field

One cannot fail to notice, when looking at shields in coats of arms, that the field can be divided in a variety of ways, and the lines so dividing the field or delineating objects appear in different forms.

The lines that divide the field are called *lines of partition*. When the lines of partition are straight, they are not mentioned in the blazon, but if any other type of line is used, it must be specified. The types of line in common use are shown in figure 13, namely, *wavy, engrailed, invected, indented, dancetté, raguly, nebuly, embattled* and *dovetailed*. Figure 14 shows straight lines with their descriptive terms and figure 15 illustrates less common lines of partition.

The lines of partition are thus used to divide the field further— so-called *methods of partition*. The lines follow the outline of any ordinary (*see* page 33), and the field thus produced is described as 'per bend', etc. Figures 16 to 22 indicate the variations that are most commonly met. In addition to these basic forms, the field may be made up of a number of 'repetitions' of

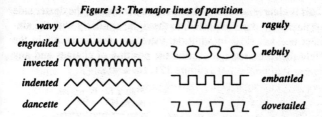

Figure 13: The major lines of partition

wavy		*raguly*
engrailed		*nebuly*
invected		
indented		*embattled*
dancette		*dovetailed*

the basic shape of the ordinary, as shown in figures 23 to 26, and the number of pieces should then be specified. Finally, some more, but not all, of the exotic methods of partition are shown in figures 27 to 29.

Wavy lines are quite common and are also called *ondé* or *undy*. These are meant to have originated from water in the same way that *nebuly* owes its origin to the shape of clouds. There seem to be few restrictions in the use of these lines, and they can be altered in wavelength and amplitude, to borrow scientific terminology, i.e. number of waves across the field and their depth. There is thus complete freedom in the number of waves used in crossing the field and the width they occupy.

Engrailed is formed from a series of connected semicircles creating pointed cusps in between, and the line is often used for the charges called ordinaries (*see* page 33), which are essentially

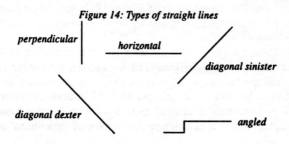

Figure 14: Types of straight lines

perpendicular

horizontal

diagonal sinister

diagonal dexter

angled

defined by straight lines. The opposite of engrailed is *invected*. The points of the partition line point outwards from the ordinary in the case of engrailed, and the opposite for invected.

Indented and *dancetté* are similar at first sight, with a serrated edge, but while indented may have any number of points, dancetté is customarily drawn with three complete 'teeth' to the full width of the field. The latter tends to be less widely used.

The line *raguly* or *ragulé* seems to be a 'relatively modern development', to quote some authorities, although it remains medieval in age. There is also debate about which way the crenellations should slant, the latter being a feature that is obviously derived from the embattled line of partition. If used in a pale or bend, the slanting crenellations should point upwards, but in a fess they could equally well point dexter or sinister.

Such doubts do not affect the *embattled* line because the crenellations (the alternative term, often used, is *crenellé*) are equally in and out about the mid-line. However, if this line is applied to the bend (a broad band going across the field) or a

Figure 15: The less common lines of partition

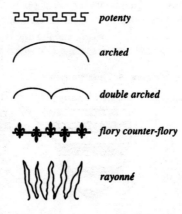

potenty

arched

double arched

flory counter-flory

rayonné

similar ordinary, only the upper line is embattled. If the lower line also shows this feature, it is called *embattled and counter-embattled*.

Dovetailed is rarely used in armory and may well be of more recent origin than raguly. The same also applies to *potenty* or *potenté*, which is obviously derived from the fur potent (*see* figure 9).

The rules of blazoning (*see* page 121) are applied when de-

Figure 16: Per fess

Figure 17: Per bend

Figure 18: Per bend sinister

Figure 19: Per pale

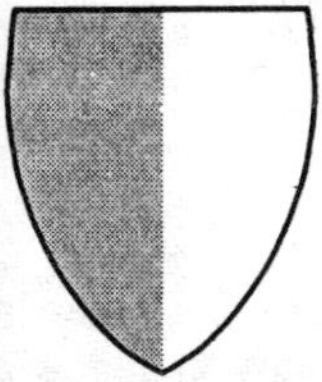

Figure 20: Per chevron

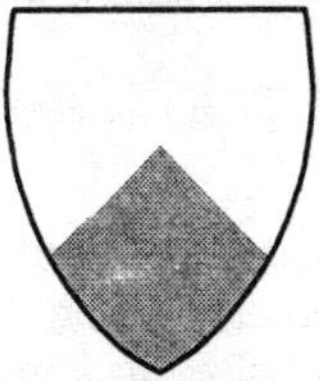

Figure 21: Per quarterly or cross

Figure 22: Per saltire

Figure 23: Barry

Figure 24: Paly

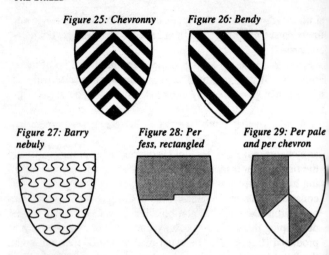

Figure 25: Chevronny

Figure 26: Bendy

Figure 27: Barry nebuly

Figure 28: Per fess, rectangled

Figure 29: Per pale and per chevron

scribing the resulting field with charges. Thus, when a field is divided, the description commences with 'per . . . or party per . . .', e.g. 'per bend arg. and purp.'. If a special line of partition is also used, it is included in the blazon, so it may be 'per bend embattled arg. and purp.'.

FURTHER SUBDIVISIONS AND TINCTURES

When a field has been divided in some manner, each division is tinctured—filled with a colour or a metal. Figure 30 shows a field *per cross* and the *quarters* have been numbered. The tincture given first, conventionally a metal, is placed in the top dexter and bottom sinister quarters (numbered 1 and 4 in the figure) to give the same tinctures diagonally opposite each other.

In the case of a pale, the tincture mentioned first falls on the dexter side of the dividing line; in fess it goes above the line. A rather interesting division of the field is *gyronny* (*see also* gyron

Figure 30: Quarters

Figure 31: A gyron (marked by the bold line)

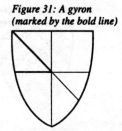

as a charge, page 55). If a field is quartered (as in figure 30) and the first quarter is then further divided per bend, then the resulting lower segment is a gyron (figure 31). The extension of this construction on to the sinister side of the shield produces a second gyron (the diagonal non-bold line in figure 31). By further developing this subdivision, a gyronny of four and more can be produced (figure 32). The usual case is that of four and eight, the latter being a quarterly division, *per saltire*. When adding tinctures to gyronny, the gyrons are tinctured alternately, so that

Figure 32: Examples of gyronny—4, 8 and 12

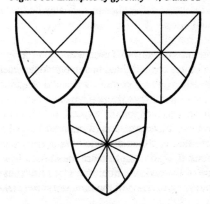

Figure 33: Examples of gyronny and the numbering of gyrons

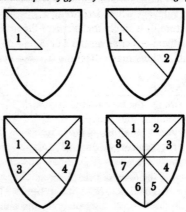

a metal and a colour are each bounded by their 'opposites'. Figure 33 shows the sequence in which tinctures are applied; however, it is permitted for both tinctures to be colour or metal.

Shields are often seen with smaller divisions, which are also called *quarters*, themselves occupying a section of a field, *per quarter* (from figure 30). Each quarter may then be quartered and the description is *quartery quartered*, or just one, two or three may be quartered. If this secondary quartering occurs, the initial quarters are termed *grand quarters*. When quarters have arms charged upon them, they are described as *quarterings*.

CHARGES

Charges on a field can occur in a variety of shapes and sizes, and although there are certain rather loose divisions, there are many exceptions or diversions from the classifications. One of the fundamental divisions, albeit far from finite, is into those charges called *ordinaries* and those called *subordinaries*.

In the main, all charges are meant to be solid and three-dimensional. This is relevant when describing a shield and applying the rule of tincture. It is likely that some of the ordinaries originated as strengthening bands on the shield and may have covered sword cuts. Others may reflect the use of a belt or scarf.

THE ORDINARIES

Otherwise known as 'the honourable ordinaries', the ordinaries can be subdivided into four groups:

> 1 bend, bar, pale
> 2 chief, fess
> 3 pile
> 4 cross, saltire, chevron

THE BEND

The bend is a wide band that crosses the shield diagonally from top left corner to bottom right, i.e. from dexter chief to sinister base (figure 34). The bend can be plain or charged and the lines can vary, adopting the styles shown already as lines of partition. If the bend crosses the shield in the opposite direction it is called a *bend sinister*. Figures 35 and 36 illustrate a *bend engrailed* and *invected* respectively. When the embattled partition line is applied to a bend, only the upper line is so ornamented. If both lines use this distinction, then it is called a *bend embattled* and *a bend embattled and counter-embattled* (figures 37 and

Figure 34: A bend

Figure 35: A bend engrailed

Figure 36: A bend invected

38). Subsequent figures illustrate a variety of other styles, although some of them, such as *bend raguly*, *bend lozengy* and *bend wavy*, are not particularly common (figures 39 to 44 show these and other variations). A bend may occur placed upon another bend, and a bend may be combined with a bordure (*see* page 51) but does not cross it.

A bend is usually placed between two or possibly four charges

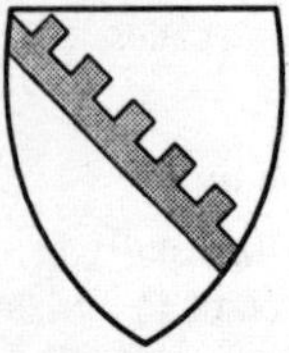

Figure 37: A bend embattled

Figure 38: A bend embattled and counter-embattled

Figure 39: A bend raguly

Figure 40: A bend lozengy

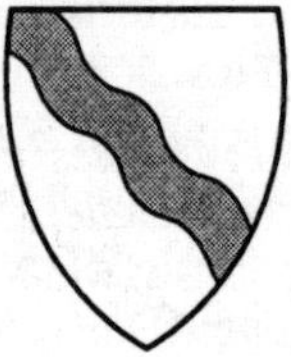

Figure 41: A bend wavy

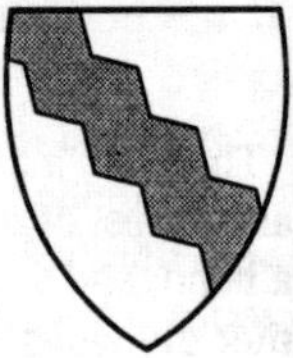

Figure 42: A bend dancetté

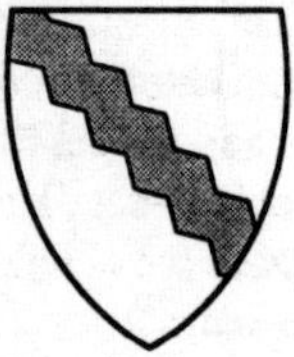

Figure 43: A bend indented

Figure 44: A bend dovetailed

and often six. The positions of the subsidiary charges (subsidiary because the bend is itself a charge) need not be specified because it is assumed that the bend separates them into two halves of equal number. Charges that are set diagonally across the field as in a bend are termed *in bend*, which is different from charges that are placed *bendwise*. *In bend* is thus where charges follow the imaginary bend line, while *bendwise* is when each charge slopes at the angle of the bend but its position on the shield is not affected.

The *bend sinister* (figure 45), which runs from the sinister chief to the dexter base, has often in the past been taken as a mark of illegitimacy but this is not commonly seen. In such cases, a derivative is used (e.g. the *baton sinister*, figure 46).

Figure 45: The bend sinister   *Figure 46: A baton sinister*

There are a number of derivatives or diminutives, i.e. subsidiary forms, of the bend. The *bendlet* is roughly half the width of a bend, and a *cotise* is half that width again. There are two further divisions. The *riband*, which is half the width of a cotise, and a *garter*, which falls between the bendlet and the cotise. However, this latter charge is very rarely encountered. It is often the case that the riband is *couped*, i.e. cut off short before it meets the edge of the shield (as with the baton sinister). Figures 47 and 48 show examples of bendlets and figure 48 also shows the bendlets *enhanced*, which is when the bendlets are raised higher than their normal position towards the chief. The derivative form of a bend sinister is called a *scarp*.

Figure 47: Bendlets

Figure 48: Three bendlets enhanced

THE BAR

The bar is very similar to the fess (*see* figure 16 and page 40), save that it is not so wide. As with the bend, it is subject to the variety of partition lines as indicated in figures 49 to 54. The bar is not placed in the fess space and is not very often used individually. Thus if there is one band it will be a fess, but two or three such pieces are bars. However, the bar is not really a diminutive form of the fess, although some authors term it such.

Figure 49: Bars engrailed

Figure 50: Two bars

Figure 51: Bars raguly

Figure 52: Bars invected

Figure 53: Bars embattled

Figure 54: Bars dovetailed

The diminutive form of the bar is called the *barrulet*, which is about half the width of the bar. A thinner version still is found, *bar gemelle* (figure 55), but this always occurs in pairs.

The size of the bars can vary and may be dictated by any charges placed on or between the bars. There is no limit to the number of bars or bars gemelles that can be placed on a shield but, in practice, there are rarely more than four. Where there is a field of bars, the number of bars is even and the tinctures applied alternately. This is called *barry of six* or *eight*. If the number exceeds eight, then the field is termed *barrulé* or *barruly*, but the particular number of bars or barrulets does not have to be quoted. If the number of bars on a field is uneven, then it must be *bars on the field* and not *barrulé*, by virtue of the arrangement of lines and application of tinctures (figure 56).

When charges are placed on the shield in a horizontal fashion, but not in fess or chief, it is termed *barwise*.

Figure 55: Two bars gemelles

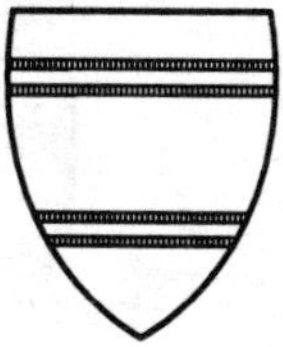

Figure 56: Arg. three bars az.

THE PALE

The pale is a band placed vertically on the shield running from top to bottom and occupying the central third of the field (figure 57). The pale is one of the four ordinaries that, being supposed to occupy one third of the field, commonly do. One occasion when the pale is so drawn, with some accuracy, is for division

Figure 57: A pale

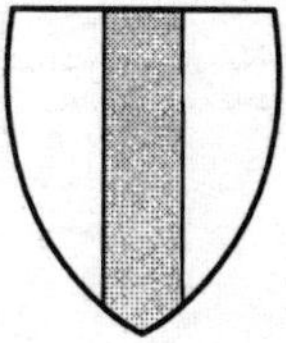

per fess and a pale counterchanged, which divides the shield into six 'equal' parts (figure 58). The diminutive form of the pale is called the *pallet* (figure 59), in which the field is termed *paly*.

Figures 60 to 65 illustrate varying forms of the pale with the different lines of partition. When the pale is cotised, it is often described as *endorsed* or just as cotised (figure 66).

Figure 58: The shield division created by a pale per fess counterchanged

Figure 59: Six pallets, producing a paly of six, arg. and gules

Figure 60: A pale embattled

Figure 61: A pale wavy

Figure 62: A pale indented

Figure 63: A pale engrailed

Figure 64: A pale dovetailed

Figure 65: A pale nebuly

Figure 66: Arg., a pale cotised az.

THE CHIEF

The chief is a rectangular, broad band that in theory fills the upper third of the shield but is commonly drawn to a smaller area (figure 67). The top edge of the chief is also that of the shield and therefore cannot be ornamented with any line of partition. The lower line of the chief, however, can be, and it is shown in various guises in figures 68 to 74. The bottom line is intended to be positioned between the honour and fess points (*see* figure 12). The edges of the chief follow the periphery of the shield as no charge is permitted to protrude beyond the sides of the shield.

The chief is very rarely *surmounted*, i.e. covered to any degree, by any other charge, and it will usually surmount all else. Occasionally, if a bordure (*see* page 51) is added later to a coat of arms as a meritorious award, then it may surmount the chief, but ordinarily the chief will surmount and cut off the bordure.

Figure 67: A chief drawn to occupy the conventional one-third of the shield

Figure 68: A chief embattled

Figure 69: A chief wavy

Figure 70: A chief engrailed

Figure 71: A chief invected

Figure 72: A chief indented

Figure 73: A chief raguly

Figure 74: A chief dovetailed

Figure 75: Gules, a chief or

The chief is never couped (shortened at its ends) nor cotised, nor does it have any common diminutive forms. There is a diminutive called the *fillet*, and Scottish heraldry does possess the diminutive *comble*. The chief cannot be carried with a fess.

If a shield shows a number of charges placed in the area where the chief would normally be, they are said to be *in chief*. A chief itself is simply described as 'a chief or', thus figure 75 shows 'gules, a chief or'.

THE FESS

The fess is a band running horizontally across the shield and occupying the middle third and drawn such that the fess point is in the middle of the band (figure 76). It cannot be featured with a chief and only one may be used on a shield—if there are two such structures, they must be bars. Figures 77 to 83 illustrate the fess with various lines of partition. The remaining lines of partition would be applied in the same way, but note that the *fess embattled* has only the upper line thus ornamented. If both lines are crenellated (as in the case of the bend, *see* figure 38), it is termed *fess embattled and counter-embattled*.

As with most ordinaries, the fess can be *cotised* (figure 84), and there are unusual and uncommon varieties illustrated in figures 85 and 86: the *fess wreathed* occurs very rarely and in figure 86 the *fess dancetté* is topped with fleur-de-lis.

Figure 76: The fess and fess point

Figure 77: A fess engrailed

Figure 78: A fess invected

Figure 79: A fess dancette

Figure 80: A fess raguly

Figure 81: A fess embattled

Figure 82: A fess indented

Figure 83: A fess dovetailed

Figure 84: A fess cotised

Figure 85: A fess wreathed

Figure 86: A variant of fess dancetté

THE PILE

The pile is a triangular, wedge-shaped ordinary that projects downwards from the top of the field (figure 87), and its angular shape and length can vary depending on the other charges required on the field or the pile itself. In its early forms, the pile almost reached the base of the shield and was not particularly wide,

Figure 87: A pile

whereas now the top edge of the pile occupies almost all the topmost line. Figures 88 to 92 illustrate the use of some of the different lines of partition with this ordinary.

The pile is a little unusual among ordinaries in that it can occur with three piles, all directed to the same point. When the three apices touch, or nearly touch, it is described as being *in point* (figure 93). A pile can originate from the base of the shield, but not singly as this would be blazoned 'per chevron'. However, in

Figure 88: A pile wavy

Figure 89: A pile indented

Figure 90: A pile embattled

Figure 91: A pile engrailed

Figure 92: A pile invected

Figure 93: Three piles in point

combination with other piles, it is possible to have one issuing *in base* (figure 94). The pile has no diminutive form.

Figure 94: Three piles, two in chief and one in base

THE CROSS

The cross is essentially formed from a pale and a fess that join at their midpoints (figure 95). It has no diminutive form but does exist in an enormous number of variations. There are probably several hundred forms of the heraldic cross, but around two dozen are found to occur most frequently. The

Figure 95: The cross

various lines of partition can be ascribed to the cross, but as a result of the diversity of this ordinary itself, not all forms are seen with different lines. Figures 96 to 100 show some of the possible variations.

Clearly the origin of the heraldic cross is the sacred cross, and when shown upon the elongated shields of those involved in the

Figure 96: A cross engrailed

Figure 97: A cross invected

Figure 98: A cross indented

Figure 99: A cross embattled

Figure 100: A cross dovetailed

holy wars, the shape would have been maintained, with a long arm 'in base'. Over time, the shield has shortened, with the resultant shortening of the long arm. Also, the use of other charges in the remaining parts of the field has led to the cross becoming a more symmetrical structure, albeit with enormous variation and flourishes.

The cross that most closely resembles the original form is, in heraldry, called a *Passion cross* (figure 101), and with Christ on the cross, it is termed a *crucifix*. The *cross Calvary* (figure 102) shows the cross placed upon a number of steps, the number of which must be specified.

Some of the more frequently encountered forms of the cross are shown in figures 103 to 105. The ordinary heraldic cross (*see* figure 95) continues to the edge of the shield unless it is couped (figure 106; notice the distinction between this and the Passion cross).

Figure 101: The Passion cross

Figure 102: The cross Calvary

Figure 103: A cross-crosslet

Figure 104: A cross moline

Figure 105: A cross patée

A cross of any form that has its base arm pointed is called *fitched* or *fitchée*. This results in an elongation of the base arm, as shown in figures 107 and 108. However, if a point is merely added to the base of an appropriate cross, such as the *cross patée*, then it is termed a 'cross patée fitched at foot' (figure 109). Other variations of the cross include the *Maltese cross* (figure 110), *Patriarchal cross* (figure 111), *St Anthony's cross* or *tau cross* (figure 112), *cross flory* (figure 113), *cross potent*

Figure 106: A cross couped

Figure 107: A cross-crosslet fitched

Figure 108: A cross patée fitched

Figure 109: A cross patee fitched at foot

Figure 110: The Maltese cross

Figure 111: The Patriarchal cross

Figure 112: St Anthony's cross

Figure 113: A cross flory

Figure 114: A cross potent

(figure 114) and *cross botonny* (figure 115). A cross that is *quarter-pierced* has the field visible in the centre where the arms meet (figure 116).

It is relatively common to see cross-crosslets scattered over a field. The term for 'scattered' is *semé*, and when applied to cross-crosslets, it is called *crusilly* (figure 117). Crusilly can also be applied to other varieties of cross arranged in this way, e.g. cross potents.

It is clear, judging from the vast number of crosses to be seen in heraldry, that many forms will have been derived from other designs, probably inadvertently because of misinterpretations and variations being introduced when artists worked from early drawings. It is said that *cross botonny* (figure 115) is such an inadvertent cross. It is considered to be an early form of the cross-crosslet, and it is easy to see how one could have been derived from the other.

Figure 115: A cross botonny

Figure 116: A cross quarter-pierced

Figure 117: Crusilly

THE SALTIRE

The shape of the saltire is well known as it is found commonly in Scottish heraldry and is known as the Cross of St Andrew, the patron saint of Scotland. It is made up of a bend and a bend sinister that join at the centre (figure 118). If they were not joined then one would lie on top of the other as separate charges.

As with the other ordinaries, the saltire can be found with different lines of partition, and figures 119 to 122 show some variations. Any charges placed on a saltire follow the slope and point to the chief, but the charge in the centre is placed upright. Charges can also be placed *in saltire*, reflecting the position of, but not found on, the saltire. If the main charge is a saltire couped, then the arms of the saltire are usually truncated parallel to the edges of the shield. An unusual variation, found also in the cross, is '. . . parted and fretty' (figure 123). If a chief occurs

Figure 119: A saltire embattled

Figure 120: A saltire invected

Figure 121: A saltire wavy

Figure 122: A saltire indented

Figure 123: A saltire parted and fretty

Figure 124

with a saltire then the latter is emblazoned, with the base of the chief forming the 'top' of the shield (figure 124).

THE CHEVRON

The shape of the chevron, an inverted V, is familiar and is possibly the most commonly occurring ordinary in British heraldry. It is the same shape as a gable rafter, and when occurring alone, the two 'legs' touch the dexter and sinister base points of the field and the apex almost touches the top of the shield (figure 125). In older forms, the chevron oc-

Figure 125: A chevron

cupies very nearly one third of the field, but in time its size diminished to allow placement of other charges, and it is usually therefore seen as a thinner band, often very similar to the lower half of the saltire. It can feature the various lines of partition (e.g. figures 126–129), and its diminutive is the *chevronel*. The

Figure 126: A chrevron engrailed

Figure 127: A chevron indented

Figure 128: A chevron nebuly

Figure 129: A chevron dovetail

Figure 130: A chevron quarterly

Figure 131: Chevron braced

chevron can also be cotised. A *chevron quarterly* is a chevron divided into two chevronels by a line *chevronwise* and a vertical line between the two apices (figure 130). The chevronel is not often seen singly but is found braced (figure 131).

This concludes the description of charges that are generally termed the ordinaries. Some authorities make no distinction between these and the next major grouping, the subordinaries. However, there is one charge that in Scotland is considered an ordinary but in England is encountered rarely: this is the pairle.

THE PAIRLE

The pairle (otherwise known as the *pall* or *shakefork*) resembles the letter Y and in its basic form is carried to the edge of the field (figure 132). A variant shown by several Scottish families is couped, with arm ends pointed, as shown in figure 133. The pairle also featured as an ecclesiastical charge in the coat of arms of an archbishop.

Figure 132: The
pairle

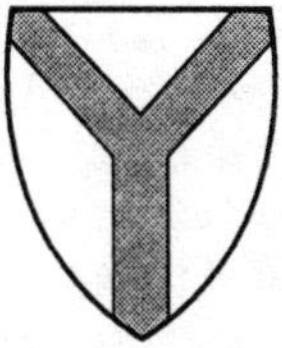

Figure 133: The pairle
couped

THE SUBORDINARIES

There are over a dozen such charges in this grouping. One distinction from the ordinaries applied by some authors is that more than one subordinary may appear in a coat of arms. However, this is not a distinction that should be scrutinized too closely, and it may be more sensible merely to regard it as a convenience when dealing with the plethora of charges and categories encountered in heraldry. There may be some argument for listing groups or classes of subordinaries where the general appearance shows some similarity, e.g. the inescutcheon, bordure, tressure and orle, or the roundel and annulet. However, these are the easier examples and other subordinaries fall less readily into such collections, thus the following descriptions appear in alphabetical order.

ANNULET

Figure 134: The annulet

The annulet (figure 134) is simply a ring and is clearly similar to the roundel, although larger. It is used regularly in heraldry, often interlaced. It is important to distinguish between an annulet and a charge of a roundel in blazoning. The surface of the annulet may be made large enough to bear small charges.

BILLET

The billet is essentially a rectangular block (and such is a wider version of it called) that stands on its shorter side (figure 135). It occurs more commonly as a field semé (i.e. strewn with) of billets, which is called *billeté* (figure 136). Neither use of the billet is very common, and for some authors it does not achieve the 'rank' of subordinary.

Figure 135: The billet

Figure 136: A field billeté

BORDURE

The bordure, as the name suggests, is a *Figure 137: A bordure* border around the edge of the shield (figure 137). It may occur plain or with charges. In the past it was used primarily as a mark of cadency (distinguishing marks between families or family members). In Scotland the bordure is never a charge and occurs as a mark of cadency. The size of

the bordure, as with many other elements of heraldry, is variable. Scottish versions tend to be wider than English ones, and a plain one is likely to be narrower than one carrying charges.

The various lines of partition can be applied to the bordure, and some examples are given in figures 138 to 141. Bordures may also be divided per pale, gyronny, and so on, and figures 142 to 146 illustrate some examples.

The *bordure wavy* (figure 138) is often used to indicate bastardy, but only in England and not in Scotland. The Scottish indication of bastardy is the *bordure compony* (figure 146). Two developments of the bordure compony do not have the same meaning: *bordure counter-compony* (figure 147) *may* mean illegitimacy, but *bordure chequy* (figure 148) has no such connotation. Note that in the latter case the boxes thus formed are not concordant with the shape of the shield.

Figure 138: A bordure wavy

Figure 139: A bordure embattled

Figure 140 A bordure indented

Figure 141: A bordure engraile

Figure 142: A bordure per pale

Figure 143: A bordure quarterly

Figure 144: A bordure gyronny

Figure 145: A bordure tierced in pale

Figure 146: A bordure compony (or gobony)

A bordure is often found with three charges but commonly the number is eight, arranged as shown in figure 149. The number of charges is stated unless it is over eight. Unusually, the rule regarding not placing colour upon colour does not always hold in the case of bordures.

Figure 147: A bordure counter-compony

Figure 148: A bordure chequy (or checky)

Figure 149: Arrangement of eight charges on a bordure

CANTON

The canton resembles a small quarter and is a diminutive of it. It occurs most commonly placed in the dexter chief (figure 150). Strictly speaking, it is meant to be one third the area of the chief, which itself occupies one third of the field; the canton thus represents one ninth of the total area. It has come to be the case that the canton does not occur with the usual array of partition lines.

Figure 150: The canton

The canton is always placed over all other charges, except where a bordure has been added subsequently, possibly as a mark of difference. In many cases the canton itself is a later addition, and when this is the case, it does not have to follow the rules governing tinctures, i.e. colour may fall on colour, metal on metal. Furthermore, if the canton covers a charge on the shield, the charge is always referred to in the blazon as if it were there. When a charge is hidden in this way, it is termed *absconded*.

A further use of the canton is an augmentation, which is usually called an augmentation of honour. This is an addition to the coat of arms, granted by the monarch to mark some distinguished action and it becomes hereditary (*see* page 143).

FLANCHES

The flanches (or *flaunches* in some accounts) comprise two curved lines, one on either side of the field. The curves are arcs of a large circle and always occur in pairs (figure 151). *Flasques* or *flasks* and *voiders* are quoted by some as alternative names while others deem them diminutives. As diminutives, they are approximately half the size of flanches.

Figure 151: Flanches

Flanches are reasonably common, and although they can exhibit the usual lines of partition, they are rarely seen to do so.

FRET

The fret is quite a common subordinary that consists of a voided lozenge (otherwise known as a mascle; *see* page 56) with which is interwoven two bendlets or ribands (i.e. thin diminutives of the bend). The ribands cross in saltire at the centre of the mascle, one crossing the mascle and being crossed by the other riband (figure 152). When the field is covered by a series of ribands and ribands sinister, in which the ribands cross over and go under each other alternately, it is termed *fretty* (figure 153). It seems that the fret may have originated from earlier coats of arms that were fretty; in some cases families with the latter now have a simple fret.

The fret usually is shown throughout (i.e. taken to the edge of the shield) when carried singly. It is sometimes seen couped when occurring as a subsidiary charge.

A *trellis* is a slight variant of fretty, in that the field is full of bendlets or ribands dexter and sinister, but they are not interwoven. In this case the bendlets lie upon the bendlets sinister where they are nailed (for which the term is *cloué*).

Figure 152: The fret   *Figure 153: Fretty*

FUSIL

The fusil is a variation of the lozenge (*see* page 56) that is narrower and longer (figure 154). For many it should not be considered a subordinary but merely another charge. Inevitably, with the latitude permitted heraldic artists in depicting charges on a shield, the delineation between the fusil and the lozenge has become somewhat blurred. However, if a number of diamond shapes occur conjoined (linked together) these will be fusils, e.g. 'az., three fusils conjoined in fess, arg.' (figure 155).

Figure 154: The fusil

Figure 155: Fusils conjoined in fess

GYRON

The gyron is not a very common charge, but does occur quite frequently as a division of the field, when a field is in gyronny (*see* pages 30–32). Figure 33 shows single and multiple gyrons and examples of gyronny. It is most uncommon to see the gyron with any of the lines of partition and although gyronny may be so ornamented, this also is to be found infrequently.

INESCUTCHEON

The inescutcheon is a shield that forms a charge on another shield. Of course, all shields are escutcheons, and the inescutcheon is only described as such when it occurs in the centre of the shield, over the fess point (figure 156). If it appears elsewhere, it is known simply as an escutcheon. Other distinctions applied are that one such charge is called an inescutcheon while more than one become escutcheons.

Figure 156: The inescutcheon

It is clear that when this subordinary is used, it might prove difficult to differentiate between a bordure (figure 137) and an inescutcheon. In fact, the bordure would normally be wide enough not to create any doubt; conversely, the inescutcheon is not usually so large that it would occupy the field left after placing a bordure. In any event, the inescutcheon should match the shape of the shield upon which it appears.

LABEL
The label has two uses, as a mark of difference for the eldest son of a family (*see* page 132) and as a charge. When the label is now seen as a charge, it may well have originated as a mark of difference. When occurring as a charge, the label is almost always placed 'in chief' and consists of a narrow band from which three short protrusions descend at right angles (figure 157). The 'prongs' of the label can take on different shapes but the dovetail is one of the more common forms (figure 158). The label may also be referred to as a *file* or *lambel*.

Figure 157: A label

Figure 158: A label with dovetail arms

LOZENGE
The lozenge is a diamond-shaped charge (figure 159) and is essentially the original form from which the fusil, mascle and rustre were derived. Furthermore, the lozenge is the shape upon which the arms of a lady or widow are displayed. Lozenges (or fusils—*see* page 56) can be found conjoined, whether in a cross

or some other form, and lozenges conjoined in a pale or a bend are called a *pale lozengy* or *bend lozengy*.

However, if the small lozenges cover the whole field, it is necessary to ensure it is not lozengy (i.e. a combination of lines bendwise and per bend sinister).

The two 'subsidiary' versions of the lozenge, the mascle and rustre, are best considered here. The *mascle* is a lozenge voided, i.e. with a central, smaller lozenge-shaped section removed, leaving only the outer border (figure 160). Mascles are common but seem to have no specific interpretation. The *rustre* is a lozenge with a circular hole at the centre (figure 161). It is rarely seen and to many ought never to be considered a subordinary.

Figure 159: The lozenge

Figure 160: The mascle

Figure 161: The rustre

ORLE

The orle is a bordure that occurs within the shield. It forms a narrow band that mirrors the shape of the shield set roughly the depth of a bordure from the edge (figure 162). It is commonly about half the width of a bordure but the dimensions vary. A similar effect can be created with an inescutcheon placed within a bordure, but the separation of the charges should indicate the correct blazon.

Figure 162: An orle

Providing the charges are not too large, they can be placed *in orle,* around the shape of the shield, and this is often referred to as 'an orle of . . . .' An orle may display the lines of partition and may itself be charged, but such occurrences are uncommon.

QUARTER

The quarter (*see* figure 30) is not frequently met, although there are some notable occurrences. In its original form, the quarter would have been just that, occupying one quarter of the shield, but the tendency has been for the size to diminish. Quarters are usually bounded by plain lines.

A more common occurrence is when a field is divided *quarterly,* and in this case the different lines of partition are more likely to be found.

The diminutive of the quarter is the *canton* (*see* page 53), and the further diminutive is the *chequer* (i.e. a small tile shape) seen in a *field chequy* (figure 163).

Figure 163: Chequeurs in a field chequy

ROUNDEL

The roundel or *roundle* is a name that includes all charges that occur as small circles of colour or metal. There is a special term for each one depending upon the tincture used. The two metals are intended to appear as flat discs while the colours are often represented as globular by means of shading (although some consider that the torteau, *see* below, should also be flat). The special names are:

> a roundel coloured gold (or) is called a *bezant*

when silver (argent) it is a *plate*
when red (gules) it is a *torteau*
when black (sable) it is a *pellet* or *ogress*
when blue (azure) it is a *hurt*
when purple (purpure) it is a *golpe*
when green (vert) it is a *pomeis*
when tenné (browny) it is an *orange*
when sangine (blood red) it is a *guze*

It is also possible to find roundels of fur. The guze, orange and golpe varieties are very rarely found, but the other forms are seen quite frequently. Roundels may contain more than one tincture, in which case it will simply be described accordingly 'per fess, of . . . and . . .'.

A further roundel that occurs quite frequently is the *fountain*. It consists of a divided field, 'barry wavy, arg. and az.' (figure 164) and is the heraldic representation for water.

Figure 164: The fountain

TRESSURE

The tressure is actually an orle gemelle, i.e. two orles, one inside the other and placed close together. It is usually quite near to the edge of the escutcheon, nearer than the orle would normally be placed. Plain tressures are virtually unheard of in British heraldry, but the *tressure flory and counter-flory* and the *tressure flory* can be found quite easily in Scottish coats of arms. These consist of fleurs-de-lis that go through the tressure.

If the heads all point out it is a tressure flory; if the heads alternate it is a tressure flory and counter-flory (figure 165).

Figure 165: Tressure flory and counter-flory

The tressure flory and counter-flory seems to have originated in the royal coat of arms and is now designated solely for such use. It cannot be granted to anyone without permission from the Crown. Some Scottish towns and cities carry the royal tressure, and a number of Scottish families claim it through female lines. In these cases it may well have been granted by augmentation (*see* page 143) rather than occurring by right through lineage.

Previous sections have dealt with the principal charges to be found in achievements, which divide the field and carry the diverse lines of partition. Not all, but most, elements have been included, and a range of partition lines have been illustrated and described to provide a grounding for an appreciation of heraldry and its interpretation.

The following sections depict the diverse array of figures, both animal and human, plants and inanimate objects, that have found their way on to the coats of arms of families and towns over the centuries.

ANIMALS AND OTHERS AS HERALDIC CHARGES

As might be expected, the number and variety of animals used as heraldic charges is quite staggering. Many mammals, birds, fish and mythical beings have, over the years, been used in coats of arms, and the way in which they have been depicted by heraldic artists has led to countless variations. In addition, there is a range of terminology depending on the stance given to the animal.

The following sections deal with the more important or common animals and their incorporation into a coat of arms. Fish, birds and animals of mythical origin are described separately. We therefore begin with animals, excluding the above mentioned groups, which incorporates a large number of mammals.

HERALDIC ANIMALS

THE LION

Among the large number of animals used, probably that included most frequently in an achievement is the heraldic lion. The lion is enormously important in heraldry and, with time, it has been depicted in an increasing number of positions. In the first instance it is likely that the shape of the shield dictated the posture of the lion, and in wishing to utilize the shield to the full, the animal was drawn upright. At this point it will be useful to introduce some of the terms adopted to describe the posture of an animal:

rampant—rearing up on the hind legs with one paw raised clawing the air

statant—standing with all four paws on the ground and facing to the right (i.e. facing dexter)

statant guardant—statant and with the head facing fully forward

statant regardant—statant and looking back over the shoulder

passant—with one foot raised; the position in which the animal is considered to be walking

sejant—sitting

combatant—two animals rampant, facing each other

couchant—lying down but with the head held upright

dormant—lying down but with the head resting and the eyes closed

salient—rampant posture but with both hind paws on the ground and the fore paws closer together. This is an uncommon position.

There are additional terms and combinations, such as *rampant guardant* and *rampant regardant*, but these will be identified as required. In the early days of heraldry, the lion was customarily upright, or rampant, and a peculiar convention was adopted whereby any lion-like animal shown as walking must be a leopard. Some adopted the ruling that, unless rampant, it would be taken as a leopard. It is likely that this confusion originated from the difficulty in distinguishing between these animals in small sketches; thus, if it was drawn passant guardant then it was a leopard became the rule. Figures 166 to 171 illustrate the basic postures.

Figure 166: A lion rampant

Figure 167: A lion passant

Figure 168: A lion passant guardant

Figure 169: A lion statant

Figure 170: A lion passant regardant

Figure 171: A lion sejant

It is customary to show the tongue and claws of a lion rampant in a colour different from that of the animal itself. The tongue and claws would normally be gules (red) unless the animal is also gules. It is stated that there is a 'lion rampant of a certain colour, armed and langued gules', i.e. the 'armed' refers to the claws (or horns, teeth, beak, talons) and the 'langued' refers to the tongue. It is considered by some unnecessary to state that the tongue and claws are armed and langued if they are red. However, any other colour used for these parts should be stated; this may happen, for example, when the lion is on a field gules.

Over the centuries, the lion has changed in its artistic representation, with the paws being drawn in different positions. Initially, the body, head and the left hind paw formed the straight, erect parts of the animal and the other paws were at angles: the left fore paw horizontal, the right angled upward and the right hind paw also angled a little upward. At this early stage (during the 13th century) there were often just three claws rather than the four now depicted.

There then followed various changes in the cycle of the paws and the attitude of the head, with gaping jaws, protruding tongue and an almost ornate tail. The variety is almost infinite, and it has to be said that some versions of heraldic lions stretch the imagination to breaking point, but there are many that are beautiful works of art.

More recent varieties have usually been drawn with the style of previous heraldic artists in mind. In addition to the terminology associated with position given earlier, there are further examples that may be met when perusing coats of arms:

rampant double-queued—when the lion is shown with two tails (figure 172), each of which comes from the base of the tail.
rampant queue-fourché—a forking of the tail, but from part way along. The tail begins at the base as a single element. It is

Figure 172: The arrangement of the tails in rampant double-queued

Figure 173: A lion sejant erect

Figure 174: A demi-lion rampant

likely that in the past this and double-queued were taken as much the same.

cowed or *coward*—this refers to when the tail is held between the legs.

sejant erect—this is a variation of sejant, in which the lion sits on its haunches, while the body is held erect with the front paws raised (*see* figure 173).

affronté—this can apply to any animal, not just the lion. It is when the animal has its whole body facing forward. This is found more in Scotland than England.

There still remains a considerable number of descriptive terms, but these are infrequently and in some cases apparently hardly ever used. Some of the less obscure terms are:

addorsed or *endorsed*—when lions are positioned back to back

counter-passant—when two lions in pale are shown passing in opposite directions (one to dexter, one to sinister)

disarmed—when a lion is represented without claws, teeth or tongue

debruised—when a lion is partly covered by another charge (although this term is not exclusive to the lion).

It is also not uncommon to see parts of a lion, either as a

charge or, as is often the case, in a crest. Probably the most common is the *demi-lion rampant* (figure 174), which is the upper half of the animal, and it can be guardant or regardant. A demi-lion is usually shown rampant and couped, thus it is assumed to be the form unless there is further qualification. Lions' heads are often seen, either couped or erased, i.e. cut off cleanly or cut off leaving a jagged edge. A lion's face may also be seen. The difference between this and a lion's head is that there is no neck showing. The lion's tail also occurs, if infrequently, as a charge or in a crest.

Finally, while considering the heraldic lion, it may be mentioned that there are a small number of 'morphological' variations, where the lion is combined with or has added to it the part of another animal. A *winged lion* is probably the most common and is usually depicted sejant (figure 175). It is often known as the *lion of St Mark*, although in its original form this beast also possesses a halo. A *sea-lion* is the upper part of a lion combined with the tail of a fish, and a *man-lion* (or *man-tiger*) features a human face.

Figure 175: A winged lion sejant

THE STAG

A common animal in British heraldry, the stag occurs almost as frequently as the lion and includes a number of variations, i.e. stag, deer, buck, hind, reindeer, and so on. The stag is represented by the male red deer with branched, pointed horns (figure 176). A buck (i.e. a fallow deer) has broad, flat horns (fig-

Figure 176: The stag trippant

Figure 177: The buck's head couped

ures 177). Whenever a stag's position is described, as with the lion, specific terms are used. Some are the same, for example statant, rampant and (sometimes) passant, but many others are different. For example, when walking it is usually referred to as *trippant* and if running, *courant* (or possibly *in full chase* or *at speed* for the latter). *Salient* is when a stag is springing, with both hind feet on the ground (similar to the position adopted by the lion). A stag is not referred to as statant guardant, as would be the case with a lion, but *at gaze*, i.e. with the face full forwards. When lying down a stag is referred to as *lodged*.

If the horns are referred to specifically, it may be said that it is 'attired of eight tynes ...', which is simply the number of points on the horns. A stag or buck is referred to as *attired*, while a goat, ram or bull is said to be *armed*. The head of the stag is also seen quite commonly, usually showing just the head, facing to the front (affronté), in which case it is called *caboshed*.

HERALDIC ANTELOPE

The ordinary antelope, should it appear on a coat of arms, will usually show the natural morphology of the animal and follow the rules established by the terms given above.

The heraldic antelope is altogether a different creature that occurs more as a supporter (*see* page 115) than as a charge. It looks quite peculiar and not in the least like the real animal, possessing as it does an ornate tail, fearsome head and jaws, and serrated horns (figure 178). It seems that this has resulted from early depictions of the antelope (or ibex) and since the real antelope was also used, the heraldic antelope came into being.

Figure 178: The head of the heraldic antelope showing the differences

FELINE CHARGES

In addition to the lion, a number of cats both large and small can be seen in heraldry. The *leopard* has been referred to already in the section on the lion, but it has its own place as a charge and not just as a default version of the lion. It is not, however, commonly seen, although the head affronté (figure 179), the head and the demi-leopard are encountered regularly. The face is also seen often and is a long-standing heraldic feature.

The *panther* occurs rarely and even then as a supporter, often with flames coming from the mouth and ears, a feature called *flammant*. In some versions, particularly those originating in Continental Europe, the panther loses any connection with reality as it assumes horns, a lion's tail, an eagle's claws and a generally ornate bearing that places it closer to the griffin (*see* page 85) than anything else.

The *tiger* is another animal that, because of its heraldic origins —when artists were depicting a creature they had probably never seen—bears little or no resemblance to the real animal. The heraldic tiger, often denoted by the spelling *tyger* or *tigre*, has a body resembling that of a tiger, although it could belong to a wolf, a lion's tufted tail, a tufted mane and legs. It possesses

Figure 179: The leopard's head erased and affronté

Figure 180: The heraldic tiger

tusks and a horn in its nose and exaggerated claws (figure 180). Because of the existence in heraldry of this monster, the more realistic representation of this species has been called the *Bengal tiger*, a distinction introduced over two hundred years ago. In fact, the Bengal tiger appears primarily as a supporter and, even then, not frequently.

The final example of the larger felines is the *lynx* (figure 181), which also occurs as a supporter rather than a charge. There are certain resemblances between the lynx and the wolf, although the latter tends to be larger, with thinner legs and a longer snout. The lynx is almost always shown *cowed*, i.e. with the tail between its legs.

The smaller *cat* or *wild cat* occurs usually in Scottish and Irish coats of arms. Also known as the *cat-a-mountain*, it is shown in figure 182.

Figure 181: The lynx

Figure 182: A cat sejant guardant

DOGS

Dogs feature quite prominently in a number of achievements, both English and Scottish. The early form of the dog is the *talbot*, a type of hound (figure 183), and this is found in the coats of arms or crests of several families. Another frequently used example is the *greyhound* (figure 184). The terminology describing the dog's position is very similar to that for other animals. It can be passant, statant, sejant and rampant; it is salient when springing with its hind feet on the ground and courant when running at full speed, but when pursuing another animal it is *in full chase*. It may also be seen lying down (couchant). Other breeds met include the bloodhound, mastiff, foxhound and spaniel.

A mythical half-breed is that of the *seadog*, which vaguely resembles a talbot but has webbed feet, a fin-like mane, some semblance of scales and a large broad tail that is very similar to that of a beaver.

Figure 183: The talbot   *Figure 184: The greyhound*

THE WOLF AND THE FOX

The wolf and the fox, which appear very similar in heraldic representations, are both quite common as supporters and charges. The wolf occurs regularly in English heraldry, but it is not particularly wolf-like (figure 185), and it resembles several other heraldic animals. This is inevitably because of poor representations by early heraldic artists, which have been perpetuated over the years. The standard terminology applies to the wolf, as it does to the fox. The fox (figure 186) is readily confused with the wolf unless it is depicted as a mask (the face affronté), in which case the vulpine features are readily recognizable (figure 187). The fox is found as a charge and as a crest.

Figure 185: The wolf

Figure 186: The fox

Figure 187: The fox mask

THE BEAR

Found quite frequently in coats of arms, the bear adopts the different positions accorded to other beasts (e.g. figures 188 and 189), and the paws may often be found in crests and as charges. Sometimes a bear will be shown muzzled, but it must be included in the blazon. The head is interesting in that its representation differs between Scotland and England. The bear's head in Scottish heraldry, when couped or erased, is truncated close behind the ears and no neck is visible. The English version includes the neck, down to the shoulders, for the same attributes (figures 190 and 191).

Figure 188: The bear passant

Figure 189: The bear rampant

Figure 190: The bear's head couped (Scottish)

Figure 191: The bear's head couped (English)

THE BULL AND OTHER BOVINES

The bull is to be found in heraldry perhaps not as frequently as a number of other animals, but nevertheless it is worthy of a mention. Because the bull naturally can be one of a variety of colours, it was never represented proper (and yet, as might be expected, there is the occasional exception to this rule). The bull occurs both as a charge (figure 192) and in a crest, and both a demi-bull and bull's head are found (figure 193).

The *ox* and *cow* feature only rarely in heraldry. However, *calves* appear in a number of coats of arms. If the horns are a different tincture from the head, a bull or cow is called *armed*, and it may be *unguled* if the hoofs are a different tincture from that of the body.

Figure 192: The bull

Figure 193: The bull's head caboshed

THE BOAR

Perhaps surprisingly, the boar is met with regularly in heraldry, as is the boar's head. There has been a distinction made in the past between the boar as a domesticated male animal and the wild boar (otherwise known as the *sanglier*), and while the sanglier occurs occasionally, in reality and practice there is no difference. The boar can be represented in the usual positions (e.g. figure 194) and, as with the lion, can be described as 'armed and langued', i.e. the tongue and claws are stated as a particular colour other than gules. The tusks are often shown in their own colour or gold. The term 'unguled' is applied in the same way as with other animals.

The distinction between the Scottish and English way of depicting the head of the bear also applies to the boar, with the Scottish boar's head truncated directly behind the ears. This distinction may have lapsed in recent years, but when considering older coats of arms it is useful. Coincidentally, the Welsh follow Scottish practice in this instance. If the boar's head is quoted to be 'borne erect', then the head is placed with the mouth pointing upwards.

Figure 194: The boar passant

THE RAM

The ram is usually but not exclusively found either statant or passant in its fairly frequent appearances in coats of arms. The ram is depicted with horns and a tail, unlike the sheep, which is shown with neither (figures 195 and 196). The *lamb*, however, also is shown with a tail. The ram can be shown armed (i.e. when the horns are a different tincture) and unguled, although this latter state is rarely seen.

A variation of the lamb is that of the *Paschal lamb* (figure 197). The lamb is quite common in Welsh coats of arms. The fleece is also seen and, naturally enough, figures more prominently in the achievement of a town or family that has strong connections with the woollen industry.

Figure 195: The ram statant

Figure 196: The sheep passant

Figure 197: The Paschal lamb

THE HORSE

The horse is a common animal in heraldry, perhaps to no great surprise, and is found passant, courant, rampant, salient and trotting (e.g. figure 198). If it is depicted with saddle and bridle, it is termed *furnished* or *comparisoned*, but if without the saddle it is *bridled*. There are also many coats in which horses form supporters.

The head of the horse may also be encountered and for no apparent reason it is often termed a 'nag's head'. Interestingly, the horseshoe is quite common, being found in the coats of a number of families, some with obvious equine connections.

Figure 198: A horse rampant

OTHER HERALDIC ANIMALS

The list of animals that can appear on an achievement seems almost endless and a few more will be mentioned here. The *goat* is a frequent occurrence and seems to be shown rampant, passant, statant or salient (figure 199). The *badger* or *brock* occurs in a few coats of arms, mainly in England. Conversely, Scotland is where most occurrences of the *otter* can be seen. The otter's head is found in a number of family coats. It may also be called a *seal's head* because the heraldic depiction is not sufficiently precise zoologically to render an identification as entirely accurate.

The *elephant* probably appears more as a supporter than as a charge, and it also features in crests. It has been used for some considerable time, but it is more often the case that the head is shown rather than the whole animal (figure 200). When shown complete, the elephant may be depicted as the *elephant and castle*, in which the castellate structure on the back of the animal represents the howdah (the canopied seat) found in India.

The *hare* is little found in British heraldry, but the *rabbit* (or, as it is usually called, the *coney*) is more common. The *squirrel* is equally common and is usually found sitting (sejant) in typical squirrel fashion.

The *hedgehog* in heraldic guise is called the *urcheon*, and it occurs in a small number of achievements, as does the *beaver*

Figure 199: The goat rampant

Figure 200: The elephant

(particularly for families with Canadian connections). The beaver is a more recent introduction (but still over 150 years old), as is the *kangaroo*, which occurs mainly as a supporter. Other animals include the bat, tortoise, porcupine, crocodile and mole —a varied selection indeed.

HERALDIC BIRDS

Heraldry has utilized many birds but, as the lion tends to dominate the other animals, so the birds are dominated by the eagle.

THE EAGLE

The eagle has long been used for its symbolism, the earliest example perhaps being that of the Roman caesars. Although it is commonly used in British heraldry, it has had far greater prominence in German heraldry, which shows some interesting features in its development. In many instances, the bird is shown spread out (or spread-eagled) and this is called *displayed* (figure 201). However, although this would be stipulated as an eagle displayed in Britain, it would simply be an eagle in German heraldry.

Over the centuries, the eagle has been shown adopting a variety of positions and various parts of the bird have been altered. The beak was, in the 13th century, closed, but by the end of the 14th was open, with the tongue visible and the head straight

Figure 201: An eagle displayed

Figure 202: A version of the eagle of Tyrol showing the sachsen

rather than raised. The claws and wings have similarly undergone changes, and the bones of the wings (called the *sachsen*) have been modified now to form a semicircle, with the feathers emanating from the bones. Figure 202 shows a typical eagle, displayed, with the sachsen visible and the claws at 45 degrees to the body. This is a relatively common feature in the coats of arms of many German provinces, cities and families. The invariably displayed eagle of German heraldry was also the case in British heraldry at the outset. However, the development of coats of arms over the last few hundred years has led to a plethora of forms and in some cases to a confusion of terminology. It is thus appropriate to look briefly at the terminology adopted in describing the eagle. The eagle displayed has already been mentioned (figure 201); the other common and generally accepted form is the *eagle close*, in which the wings are flat against the body and the bird is standing (on the ground) (figure 203). The clearest descriptions beyond these two are probably to be found in Fox-Davies' works. There is advocated the use of the word 'rising' followed by any specific terms that are necessary for the blazon. Figures 204 and 205 show two such examples. *Volant* is the term used for a bird that is flying. If no position is specified for a bird in the blazon, it is taken that it is close. As with other charges, if the head or a limb is shown cut

Figure 203: An eagle close

Figure 204: An eagle rising

Figure 205: Alternative version of the wings of an eagle rising

off, it is called *erased* if the edges are jagged, and *couped* if cut off cleanly.

The *double-headed eagle* (figure 206) has occurred for many, many years, although its origin has been the subject of some debate. It seems logical to assume that this form existed before being used in heraldry. In the early days of heraldry the single and double-headed eagle were probably used indiscriminately, and then the double-headed version was adopted as the Imperial sign. It was certainly used in early times and by the Holy Roman and German empires in the 14th and 15th centuries.

When an eagle is shown with its beak in a different colour, it is termed *armed*, and it is called *membered* when the legs differ in this way. The head, wings and leg are often seen as charges or crests. Pairs of wings are also seen, whether joined (termed *conjoined in leure* if they meet at the base: figure 207) or separate (although in the latter case they are usually *not* called a pair). When single wings are shown, it is assumed to be the dexter wing that is used. Legs are usually erased at the thigh, which is termed *erased à la guise*, and if shown couped below the line of the feathers, it is then more accurately called a claw.

Figure 206: General shape of a double-headed eagle	*Figure 207: Wings conjoined in leure*

THE MARTLET

The martlet is, rather surprisingly, quite a common bird in heraldry. It is the heraldic version of the swallow, but it is always shown without feet and usually without legs. This curious form probably originated in the past belief that a swallow cannot perch and spends all its time flying because of this morphological inadequacy! It is rare, although not impossible, to see a swallow alight or settle on the ground, but this is clearly the origin of the martlet's heraldic representation. The martlet is also used as the mark of cadency for the fourth son, the connection being that, in the distribution of the parents' land to their offspring, by the time the fourth son is reached, there will be no land left upon which he can stay. Figure 208 shows a martlet volant.

Figure 208: A martlet volant

A number of other birds found in heraldry are considered briefly below, but this list is by no means exhaustive.

THE DOVE

The dove seen in heraldry often manifests an ornithological peculiarity, a tuft on top of the head (figure 209). A common occurrence of the dove is with an olive branch in its beak, but it is

Figure 209: The dove

equally seen depicted as a *dove close* and with a laurel branch in its beak. It is also seen as a *dove rising*, in which it has outstretched wings and is flying.

THE FALCON

The falcon was obviously important in earlier times in the pursuit of falconry, and so it is not surprising that it features quite strongly in heraldry. There is no distinction made between the falcon and the *hawk*, but the bird may be named specifically in the case of *allusive* arms (also *canting* or *armes parlantes*), i.e. where the bird alludes to the name or profession of the family.

Also linking the falcon with its past role is the likelihood that it will be shown *belled*, i.e. with a bell on either or both feet. There is little consistency in this matter, and several versions of the terminology can be found. In some cases 'belled' refers to a bell on either or both feet, in which case it is also *jessed* (the jess being the leather strap that attaches the bell to the leg). Alternatively, 'belled' may also be used to describe a falcon with bells on both legs, because a falcon must be assumed to always be belled (i.e. on at least one leg). It is usually the case that two bells are drawn (figure 210), but if the bells and jesses are of different colours, then of course the terms 'belled' and 'jessed' should be used.

A falcon may be shown *armed*, specifying a different colour for the legs and beak, but it has become common practice to use

Figure 210: Detail of a falcon showing the bells

the term *beaked and legged* when these are a different tincture from the body. Since it was practice in falconry to hood the bird while it was on the wrist, it is not surprising that *hooded* refers to the bird when it is shown blindfolded. Also linked to falconry, is the depiction of the bird with its prey. When it is preying on another animal, it is sometimes said to be *trussing its prey*, although 'trussed' means with closed wings, so there is scope for further confusion here.

THE OSTRICH

Ostrich feathers are commonly used in heraldry and the bird itself is frequently encountered, albeit more as a crest than a charge. It is usually shown 'proper', unlike many other birds, which have departed from their natural form beneath the hand of the heraldic artist. There is, however, one strange manifestation of the ostrich—it is quite often depicted (particularly in older coats of arms) holding a metallic object in its beak. This could be a key, horseshoe or something similar.

THE OWL

The owl is quite a popular bird heraldically and it is commonly shown in the pose naturally adopted by the bird, i.e. with the face affronté.

THE PEACOCK

One might expect that the beautiful plumage of the peacock would be employed in heraldry, and that is indeed the case. Also, it would be strange not to employ the full grandeur of the bird's tail, so it is usually shown affronté with the tail fully displayed and this is termed *in his pride*.

THE PELICAN

The pelican undergoes a curious change from its natural to its heraldic form. It is customarily shown in a particular position, which is called *a pelican in her piety*. This shows the bird standing in the nest with her young and with the head bowed so that the beak is pecking at the breast. This is called *vulning herself*, and the drops of blood falling from the wound provide nourishment for the young (figure 211). If this were not strange enough, the bird thus depicted is shown with the beak, and to a certain extent the upper body, of an eagle. If the head of the pelican is shown, it also maintains this peculiar position. In most cases, when blazoned 'proper', it shows not the natural white colour but that of the eagle. However, more recent usage has adopted its natural colour and posture, including the characteristic pouched beak.

Figure 211: A pelican in her piety

THE RAVEN
The raven is heraldically rarely distinguished from the rook and the crow. It has a long history of use in heraldry and can be seen in very early coats of arms.

THE SWAN
The swan is commonly found as a crest and as a charge, in the latter case in a variety of positions. As a charge it is commonly found as a *swan close* but can also be regardant, rising and, in some cases, swimming.

The foregoing are just a small number of the many birds that feature in heraldry. There are many others, including the *duck* (with some varieties); the *heron*, which often has an eel in its beak; the *stork*, which similarly can have a snake; the *parrot* or, as it is termed in heraldry, the *popinjay*; the *lapwing* (and its alternative names); the *magpie* and even the *vulture* can be found, in one instance as supporters.

THE USE OF FEATHERS

Feathers are found occasionally as charges, in particular ostrich feathers. Crests are likely to feature feathers more frequently, derived no doubt from the helmets worn at tournaments where the owners' crests were not borne but simply a plume of ostrich feathers. The plume has therefore been 'adopted' into the crest of a number of families. The number of feathers in a plume is usually stated and is commonly three, five or seven. Although generally white, the feathers can be shown coloured, which may require careful blazoning. When the colours are mixed, the feather on the extreme dexter is described first, and this applies whatever the number of colours, working from dexter to sinister and back again.

Peacock's and cock's feathers are also found, but ostrich is the commonest. The way in which the feathers are represented has differed through time, ranging from an erect, rather rigid format to a more realistic, drooping shape—and back again.

Crests are considered on page 106.

HERALDIC FISH

It will have become clear that heraldry tends to pay little heed to animal form and appearance, and it will therefore come as no surprise to learn that taxonomy and classifications are also given scant consideration. The use of fish in heraldry thus encompasses not only fish in the strict sense but also whales, dolphins and other sea creatures, including lobsters, crabs and even certain shells. When fish appear as charges, it is usually the case that no distinctive features are shown to enable them to be identified; it is simply the generic form of a fish that is represented.

When a fish is shown on a shield in a horizontal position, it is called *naiant*, irrespective of whether it is in the water or not. If the fish is placed vertically on the shield, it is called *hauriant* (figure 212). In this case, the head is usually placed to the top, but this does not necessarily follow, and it is customary to state whether the head is upwards or downwards.

Fish tend not to appear very frequently in heraldry, but it is possible to find the *salmon*, which features in the coats of arms of Glasgow and Peebles. The *herring*, *roach* and *trout* are all seen, if only occasionally. The *pike* occurs under a number of alternative names, including jack, lucy (in English heraldry) and ged (in Scotland). These last two terms make an obvious connection with certain families such as Lucy, Lucas and Geddes. Pyke is an obvious family name in this case.

Other charges include the *eel*, which features in the arms of Ellis, the *perch*, *crayfish*, *cod*, *flounder*, *mackerel*, *prawn* and others.

Probably the most interesting and common of the 'fish', which of course is not a fish, is the *dolphin*. The heraldic form of the dolphin bears only passing resemblance to the creature itself (figure 213), and there is a very considerable variation in the forms presented. The dolphin seems to have a long heraldic history and its prominence in Europe probably derives from its connection with the dauphins of France.

Figure 212: A fish hauriant   *Figure 213: The heraldic dolphin*

HERALDIC REPTILES

Within this category there are few charges to be found and the creature encountered most frequently is the *serpent* (in various guises). *Lizards* occur occasionally, but it is likely that other occurrences, e.g. *frogs*, are mistakes or misrepresentations.

When a serpent is seen, it is usually intertwined upon itself, a position called *nowed* (figure 214). It was the case in the past that the interlacing followed a particular pattern, but this is no longer necessarily adhered to. The serpent or snake may also be found erect and is also found *glissant* (gliding). It appears relatively frequently in British heraldry because of its connection with the symbolic representation of medicine, and it is therefore not surprising to see it in the coats of arms of medical organizations and practitioners.

Figure 214: A serpent nowed

HERALDIC BEASTS

The imagination appears to have been given complete freedom when the array of heraldic beasts and monsters is considered. However, most bear a passing resemblance to one or more natural animals, although the more elaborate creatures tend to have featured and to remain in the history of heraldry. Many of these creatures are hybrids of two animals, although in some cases the link to any semblance of reality is rather tenuous. Even then, it is possible to see the origin of the dragon in the existence of the crocodile and the iguana.

THE DRAGON

There are many similarities between the dragon and the griffin, although on closer scrutiny it is seen that these are merely superficial likenesses. The essential features of a dragon are the body covered with scales (apart from the breast), webbed claws, wings that resemble those of a bat, and a tongue and tail that are both barbed.

The head is quite unique in heraldry, with scales on the neck, an open mouth with barbed tongue, and pointed ears. It is difficult to see where its origin can be placed, save in a highly fertile imagination. The legs are scaled and clawed, and the underside of the body shows not as scales but as folds, which may be larger scaly features. The wings are interesting in that they are always represented as those of a bat, with the bony ribs across the full depth of the wing. It is a very graphic and impressive creature (figure 215), and although it is not extremely common, it does occur in the coats of arms of a number of eminent families, including royalty. A dragon is usually shown statant, rampant or passant and occasionally couchant.

Figure 215: A dragon

THE GRIFFIN

The griffin (or alternatively the *gryphon*) is often regarded as the typical heraldic monster. It is a hybrid, combining the head and claws of an eagle with the body, hind legs and tail of a lion. The claws of the eagle then act as the forepaws (figure 216). It possesses the wings of an eagle (which are never shown *close*, i.e. down flat on the body), and it also has ears. If one should see a griffin's head erased, then the ears are the only means by which it can be distinguished from an eagle (figure 217).

It is usually coloured in some manner that would be considered different from proper (i.e. brown plumage with the natural colour of the lion), and commonly the beak and claws are shown in a different colour from the rest of the body. It may then be described as *armed*, although it may also be called *beaked* and *fore-legged* when differentiated in this manner.

A griffin may be found in the range of positions that would be expected for a lion, except, according to some authorities, in the one case of rampant. When a griffin occupies this position it is termed by some *segreant*.

The griffin is quite well used in heraldry, and the *demi-griffin* is often found as a crest. Similarly, the griffin's head is commonly found as a charge. There is also a *male griffin*, which differs from the version shown in that it has no wings. It does, however, possess spikes at various points of the body (figure 218). This is not a common charge. An interesting, but very rarely seen, variation of the griffin is the *opinicus*. It is very similar to the griffin but the body resembles that of a lion with a modest tail somewhat like that of a camel. The eagle's head is present, and the feathers cover the neck and upper breast, and the full wings are displayed.

Figure 216: The claws/ forepaws of the griffin

Figure 217: A griffin's head erased

Figure 218: The griffin

THE UNICORN

This animal, long the subject of fairytale and fable, is drawn with the body of a horse, the legs and feet of the deer, and the tail of the heraldic lion. The head, that of a horse, is modified by a beard and the long, twisted horn so characteristic of the image. It tends to possess a long flowing mane, matching the flourish of the tail (figure 219). It can adopt the customary positions (rampant, passant, statant, etc). It may be shown with the mane a different colour from the body, in which case the term *crined* is used, although this is met more frequently with respect to the hair of human figures.

It seems that most versions of the unicorn through history may have emanated from the account of Pliny, the Roman naturalist, who described it as a ferocious beast with the body of a horse, the head of a deer, the feet of an elephant and the tail of a boar. It also had a deep bellowing voice and, of course, a single (black) horn in the middle of its forehead. Although this is somewhat different from the heraldic representation of the unicorn, it may have had something to do with this creature's presence in the subject.

Figure 219: The unicorn

PEGASUS

Pegasus is, of course, another equine and features quite commonly in heraldry of more recent days. In the lore of Greek mythology, Pegasus came into being as a result of Perseus cutting off the head of the Medusa. The blood drained into the earth, from which arose Pegasus. Minerva then caught and tamed Pegasus and presented him to the Muses (the daughters of Jupiter and Mnemsoyne), who were supposed to preside over song and prompt the memory. Thus Pegasus was at the behest of poets, but in heraldry, because its form suggests swift flight (figure 220), it has to some extent become associated with families involved with hunting or horse racing.

Figure 220: Pegasus

THE PHOENIX

The phoenix is very similar to the eagle save that it is always depicted rising out of flames (figure 221). Also, when represented in colour, the plumage is more colourful than that of the eagle. It is not especially common as a charge but does occur as a crest. It is customarily shown as a demi-bird, and although the flames ('. . . issuant from flames of fire . . .') are usually mentioned in the blazon, this is not essential.

The phoenix is, of course, another creature of Greek mythol-

Figure 221: The phoenix

ogy, described by Ovid as a being that reproduces itself and lives on frankincense and odoriferous gums. It supposedly lives for five hundred years, at the end of which time it builds a nest in the branches of an oak or on top of a palm tree and, having surrounded itself with cinnamon, myrrh and other spices, it expires. A young phoenix then emerges. The historian Tacitus provides further details of the bird revisiting Egypt after a sustained absence, and it may be from his account that the image of the flames comes. The account says that the young bird takes up the body of his father and flies with it to the altar of the sun. There it is left to be 'consumed in flames of fragrance'.

THE COCKATRICE

The cockatrice (sometimes called the *basilisk*) is another wonder of mythology that has found its way into the heraldic library. It was called the king of the serpents, signified by the comb or crown on his head. The cockatrice was supposed to have been created from the egg of a cock hatched by a toad or serpent on a dunghill. There were several varieties, one burning up anything that approached and another causing a look of horror followed by death. Not surprisingly, it is not a particularly attractive creature (figure 222). Nor does it occur commonly in heraldry, and less so as a charge than a crest.

Figure 222: The cockatrice

THE WYVERN

The wyvern or *wivern* is very similar in its upper body to the dragon. The head and ears are almost identical, as are the forelimbs and wings. However, the lower body narrows into a tail with a barbed end. It is usually depicted resting upon its tail and legs, although it may be seen erect ('standing' upon its tail with claws in the air). The wyvern is not particularly common, although in other countries it is seen more often but under the name of a dragon.

Figure 223: The head of the wyvern (it has the body of the dragon)

THE SPHINX

The Sphinx in Egyptian and Greek mythology was a creature that preyed upon the town of Thebes. It lay on a rock by the roadside and to every passing traveller posed a riddle. If the traveller failed to solve it, he or she was doomed, while a solution led to a safe passage. No one succeeded in solving the riddle until Oedipus one day approached the Sphinx. He was able to solve the riddle, whereupon the Sphinx threw herself from the rock and perished.

In heraldry, the Sphinx is the customary hybrid of lion and woman, with the body, legs and tail of the former and the breasts, head and face of the latter. It is not a common charge but is to be seen in a number of coats of arms.

THE CENTAUR

A similar sort of hybrid, the centaur is man and horse. The man shows from the head to the loins, and the remainder of the body is that of the horse. It is not uncommon, although it appears more in Continental European than in British heraldry. It occurs in several family crests and occasionally as a supporter.

The centaur was, by comparison with other mythical beings, relatively favoured and was commonly allowed into human society. On his death, the wisest of all centaurs, Chiron, was placed among the stars of the constellation Sagittarius by Jupiter.

OTHER MYTHICAL BEASTS

There are a number of other mythical beasts and beings, including the *mermaid*, the *apres* (a bull with a bear's tail), the *musimon* (an heraldic goat with a ram's head and an extra pair of horns) and the *mantygre* (a lion with a man's head, with straight horns).

Finally, a rarely used and noxious creature, albeit interesting, is the *harpy*. It is a hybrid of the vulture with the head, neck and breasts of a woman, and seems to occur more in German heraldry. It seems to have its origin in the adventures of Aeneas, who found these creatures on the island of Harpies. The harpies had been sent by the gods to torment a certain Phineus, who had been punished by Jupiter because of his cruelty.

THE HUMAN FIGURE AS USED IN HERALDRY

The human figure, or parts of it, occur extensively in heraldry, although the majority of cases are probably as supporters or in crests. There are instances of *Christ on the Cross*, the *Virgin Mary with Child* and a *demi-figure* of the Virgin, and in the main these occur in the crests or coats of arms of towns and burghs. *Saints* feature in a number of Scottish coats of arms, and *Biblical characters* appear quite frequently in Continental European coats. Figures of all sorts and in a variety of dress can be found as supporters but are too numerous to mention individually.

Parts of the body are commonplace—be it a head, arm, hand or leg. The *head* features on a number of coats, and there are instances of Saracens, Saxons, old men, savages and others, but the Saracen, moor and savage seem to have dominated in the past. The head of a woman is usually shown as being young and beautiful and commonly with golden hair. When the hair is coloured differently then the term *crined* is applied.

Hands are seen frequently and are stated to be dexter or sinister (figure 224). They are taken to be couped at the wrist. If the hand is open with the palm visible, it is called *apaumé*. The *arm* may be used in a number of positions: two thirds of the forearm, not quite to the elbow and with the hand clenched, is called a *cubit arm*; an arm couped at the elbow reveals more of the arm but is rarely used; and when all the arm from shoulder to fingers is used, it is always bent at the elbow and is called *embowed*. This may be shown with the fingers pointing to sinister (figure 225) or to dexter (then called 'arm embowed to the dexter'), and it may even be placed on the point of the elbow ('an arm embowed fesseways'). Two arms juxtaposed is called *counter-embowed*, and if interlinked, it is *counter-embowed and interlaced*. If the arm is bare it is called *proper*, but if clothed it may be *habited* or *vested*, or if in armour then it would be blazoned 'an arm embowed in armour'.

Figure 224: A sinister hand   *Figure 225: An arm embowed*

BOTANICAL CHARGES

There are many instances of trees, leaves, flowers, fruit and even some vegetables being used on shields. Some come to mind immediately, such as the fleur-de-lis, the trefoil or the heraldic rose, and these are considered in due course.

TREES AND LEAVES

There is considerable use made of trees in heraldry and, although there may not be much differentiation pictorially, the names are usually specified carefully as they often have a definite link with the family name. If the roots of a tree are shown, it is called *eradicated*, but if it is shown growing out of the ground, it is termed 'issuant from a mount vert'. The tree seen most frequently is the *oak*, but a veritable forest of varieties has been used in the past, including *maple*, *cypress*, *ash*, *coconut*, *cedar* and *fir*. *Branches* and *trunks* may also be found; in fact, the latter have played quite a prominent role in the past.

Several varieties of leaves may be encountered, including *oak*, *vine*, *maple* (especially for those with Canadian connections), *hazel* and *bay*. The *trefoil* (and other forms to be mentioned) is theoretically a leaf but it and its derivatives (the *quatrefoil*, *cinquefoil*, and *octofoil* or *double quatrefoil*) tend to be placed

Figures 226–228: The trefoil, the quatrefoil and the cinquefoil

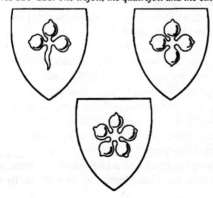

in a group by themselves because they are recognized as being exclusively heraldic charges. The trefoil is always shown with its stalk (figure 226), which is termed *slipped*, but it is usually considered not necessary to mention it in the blazon. The trefoil has undoubted similarities with the Irish shamrock, from which it was presumably derived. The quatrefoil consists of four 'leaves' arranged symmetrically but occurs only rarely. A more frequent version is the cinquefoil, which not surprisingly contains five leaves (figure 228). Both the quatrefoil and cinquefoil do not usually occur slipped. The cinquefoil was used a great deal in early coats of arms, and it is highly likely that this charge actually had its origin in the shape of a flower.

FLOWERS

A number of flowers are found as heraldic charges, including the lily, poppy, tulip, marigold, thistle and sunflower, and these will be considered in due course. Probably the best known are the heraldic rose and the fleur-de-lis.

The *fleur-de-lis* (figure 229) has its origin in what was the arms of France. It is meant to represent the lily (iris family) but there are many suggestions as to how it developed and came to occupy its place in heraldry. It has many connections with royalty and is met with quite frequently in the coats of arms of towns.

The *heraldic rose* is seen quite often in English heraldry, and in its simplest form was drawn with five petals and, in effect, displayed (figure 230). It is a fairly good representation of the wild rose seen in hedgerows, with the spaces between petals shown. However, subsequent varieties are often seen with two rows of petals. When the rose is shown in its natural colours it is termed 'barbed and seeded proper' or 'barbed vert and seeded or', referring to the green calyx and yellow-coloured seeds. As with the trefoil, the term *slipped* is used when the stalk is

Figure 229: The fleur-de-lis   *Figure 230: The heraldic rose*

shown. However, it is customary also to show a leaf, and a 'rose slipped and leaved' would have two leaves, one on either side of the stalk. The heraldic rose is quite common on military badges and is, of course, associated with the counties of Yorkshire and Lancashire.

After the heraldic rose, the *thistle* is probably one of the most important flowers in British heraldry. It first appeared in the coinage of James III of Scotland, around 1474, and subsequently became one of the recognized emblems of Scotland in the mid-16th century. It is generally shown as the conventional flower on a short stalk and with a leaf on either side, and it is usually depicted proper.

Although the *lily* features mostly as the fleur-de-lis, it can be seen in its own right, particularly in the coats of arms of some colleges. The other flowers mentioned above do not occur very frequently but, when they do, are often depicted proper.

FRUIT

Fruit is rarely seen in British heraldry, although there are occasional references to *apples*, *pears* and *oranges*. *Pineapples* are also mentioned but these are really fir cones. The fruit of the oak, the *acorn*, is also seen, often slipped and leaved (figure 231).

The final charge to mention in this section is the *garb*. This is the term for a sheaf of grain, and its use can be traced back a very long way, to around the 13th century. Garbs are associated with the coats of arms of families who held land under the feudal system. Unless it is specified otherwise, a garb is taken to be a sheaf of wheat. It is usually shown *banded*, i.e. with a cord binding it (figure 232).

Ears of wheat, rye and other grain are also quite common in British heraldry.

Figure 231: An acorn slipped and leaved

Figure 232: A garb

THE USE OF OBJECTS IN HERALDRY

There is quite an array of inanimate objects used in heraldry, from buildings such as towers to weapons, buckles, chess pieces, stars and other items with a specifically heraldic origin.

Here we look at a reasonable selection of such items. This list is by no means exhaustive but includes those objects that either occur more frequently or about which more is known.

Among buildings, an *abbey* is sometimes seen, or in some cases a *monastery*, and in one coat of arms a ruined abbey is featured. Bearing in mind the nautical history of England, it is not surprising that the *anchor* is seen quite frequently (figure 233). *Arrows* and *arrowheads* are used quite often in heraldry. Another version of the arrowhead, which has a barbed head engrailed on the inner edge, is called a *pheon* (figure 234). If the inner edge is not engrailed, then the charge is called a *broad arrow*.

Figure 233: An anchor

Figure 234: A pheon

Figure 235: A square buckle

Bells are found both here and on the Continent, and, unless stated otherwise, it is assumed to refer to a church bell. However, hawks' bells are seen. Sometimes the striker of the bell (the clapper) is coloured differently from the bell itself. A rather more common charge is the *buckle*, which occurs in a variety of shapes. It may be square, circular or lozenge-shaped (e.g. figure 235) and also oval and occurs in British and Continental European heraldry. The lozenge-shaped buckle seems to be more common on the Continent.

An interesting charge is the *caltrap*, which is a representation of a military instrument. It was made of iron and was used to annoy the cavalry of the enemy. It consists of four spikes with each point at the apex of a tetrahedron (figure 236). This ensured that however the implement was thrown to the ground there would always be a spike uppermost. An alternative name for this, not surprisingly, is the *cheval trap*.

Chains are just mentioned: they are seen rarely in British heraldry and when they do occur usually form part of a crest. Chains as a charge do feature more in Continental heraldry.

The *crescent* is seen quite frequently and features as a charge and as a difference (i.e. a figure or mark used to differentiate between families and to show the distance between them, *see* page 133). The crescent is essentially the crescent moon depicted with the 'points' turned upwards (figure 237), but it can also be

Figure 236: A caltrap

Figure 237: A crescent

Figure 238: An escallop

used with the opening facing dexter (*increscent*) or sinister (*decrescent*). In the use of the crescent as a difference mark, it us used to signify the second son.

A fairly frequent charge on ecclesiastical coats of arms is the *crosier*, the pastoral staff of a bishop or abbot. It also occurs in the coats of some families but it is not a frequent occurrence.

The *escallop* is perhaps one of the most widely employed charges in many countries. In the days of pilgrimages to the Holy Land, escallops were worn by the palmers (the pilgrims who went to Palestine and returned with a palm branch or leaf) as a sort of badge. They then probably found their way on to the shields of some families involved with the Crusades and thereafter by others who had no such connection.

A seemingly peculiar charge to see, although items of warfare are common in heraldry, is the *bomb* or *grenade*. It is depicted somewhat differently from its modern counterparts (figure 239) but does occur in the arms of a number of families.

The *maunche* or *manche* is the heraldic term for the old-fashioned sleeve, which is a capacious flowing part of dress. It is often drawn as to be almost unrecognizable (figure 240) and had its origin in the 'favour' of a lady's sleeve.

Numerous bladed weapons have been taken into coats of arms, and the *seaux* is an interesting example. It is a handled blade, curved like a scimitar with a notch on the back edge of the blade

Figure 239: A bomb or grenade

Figure 240: The maunche

Figure 241: The seaux

(figure 241). The *scimitar* itself, *sabre* and *cutlass* may all appear in coats of arms.

Ships are used, in their various guises, in the coats of arms of a number of families. One vessel, the *galley* or *lymphad*, occurs commonly in the arms of West Highland clans (figure 242). A number of towns also have a galley in their arms. Other sailing vessels that may be seen include a *yacht* or a *steamer*, and even the *ark* is found in a small number of families.

Returning to the theme of battles and weapons, *spears* are commonly found. These occur as the *lance* or *javelin* (figure 243) and the slightly different *tilting spear* (figure 244). The latter derives from a variety of jousting, called the tilt, in which a wooden barrier (also called the tilt) separated the combatants. The barrier was quite high (about 5 feet or 1.5 metres) and ensured that there were no collisions. It also helped prevent a

Figure 242: The lymphad

Figure 243: The lance or javelin

Figure 244: The tilting spear

fallen rider being trampled by the other horse. Tilting armour was strengthened on one side to give greater protection if struck with the tilting spear in a joust. *Spurs* are also seen in a few coats, particularly in branches of the Knight family, e.g. 'on a spur in fess, a hawk statant', and 'on a spur, in fess or, an eagle, per fess arg. and az., wings expanded of the first, beaked and legged gu.'.

Possibly the most numerous charge in this vein is the *sword*. There are several variations, including a single sword, a flaming sword and a sword entwined by a serpent. A sword is often seen held aloft by a hand or in a paw of some description. The sword is standard in its representation, while a *dagger* has a shorter blade that is more pointed. If weapons are shown spotted with blood, they are called *imbrued*.

Celestial bodies, i.e. the sun and other stars, feature quite prominently in heraldry. There are basically three types of *star*. It is unusual in English heraldry to find this charge called by the name 'star', but should it occur it would have six points or rays, and it is usually shown as argent (e.g. for the family name Alston or Alstone: 'a star or, on a crescent arg.'; and 'a star, proper'). The number of rays must be specified if there are more than six. It is drawn as a conventional star. If the rays of the star are wavy, it is called an *estoile* or *etoile* (from the French, meaning 'star'). The estoile may be seen with six wavy rays (figure 245) or it may have eight points with half wavy and half straight. The estoile is not usually shown pierced. One of the

Figure 245: An estoile

Figure 246: The mullet

coats for the family Baillie in Scotland is '. . . out of clouds proper, an etoile of eight points, or'.

The *mullet* (from the French *molette*, meaning the rowel or spiked revolving disk of a spur) is a five-pointed star (sometimes called the *Scottish star*). A mullet of more than five points must have the number stated. It may be plain (figure 246) or pierced, i.e. with a small hole in the centre, in which case it is sometimes called a *spur revel* or *spur rowel*.

The *sun* when represented heraldically is shown with numerous rays that commonly alternate, straight and wavy. It is frequently shown also with a human face and is blazoned 'a sun in its splendour'. A similar description for the moon would be 'in her complement'.

Numerous architectural features may be found in coats of arms, including castles, arches and towers. A *castle* usually comprises two towers joined by a section of wall containing the entrance gate (figure 247). A *tower* also has an entrance gate (figure 248). Some coats with such charges include Rawson ('a falcon sa., rising from a tower or; a castle sa., flagged, gu.') and Rawston ('out of a ducal coronet, a demi-lion rampant, supporting a tower, triple-towered). *Triple-towered* is the term used when a tower or castle is topped by smaller towers.

There are many more objects that appear as charges, if only rarely, from further weapons (including scaling ladders) to torches, cups, cushions and keys.

Figure 247: The castle   *Figure 248: The tower*

THE HELMET, CROWN AND CREST

The helmet has undergone numerous transitions from its earliest appearance before the Norman conquest, through the development of metal armour and the addition of all sorts of embellishments. Heraldry has used what most would consider to be the conventional picture of a helmet, as worn by a knight, but in many cases the pictorial representation depicted is quite unrealistic and could never be worn. Nevertheless, the helmet does add a degree of distinction to a coat of arms. It is useful to consider, briefly, the major phases and styles in the development of helmets over the years.

Leather or linen was the material first used for protection, but around the time of the Norman Conquest, metal was introduced. A padded cap would be worn on the head, over which was placed the helmet. The helmet worn by Norman soldiers was roughly conical in shape and comprised a number of metal plates riveted together. This created an iron hat to which was attached a guard piece for the nose, called the *nasal*. Subsequently, ear guards were added, and the *barrel helm* developed from the joining of these guards to form something resembling the shape of a tin can. Slots allowed the wearer to see, albeit in a somewhat limited fashion, and breathing was effected through small holes. These openings were called the *occularium* and the *ventoil* respectively. It was important in battle not to present a flat surface against which a blade could strike with effect. Thus the earlier flat top of the barrel helm soon developed sloping surfaces, but even then, the helmet did not rest on the shoulders, and it must have been very difficult to keep it in place.

The *great helm* superseded the barrel helm in the late 13th century and lasted for some time as it was stable, being fastened to the shoulders. The main problem with such helmets must have been their weight. In many cases they were made of *cuir bouilli*, which is leather, boiled in water or oil, that is then shaped. Upon drying, it became rock hard but was much lighter than metal.

The next development consisted of a metal cap, the *bascinet*, worn over a hood made of mail (the *camail*) (figure 249). Visors were subsequently added to protect the face, and the camail was fastened to the bottom of the cap and draped over the shoulders. The bascinet was followed by a number of helmets, each with essentially the same principle, that of a more complete coverage but also affording protection for the neck. The *schallern* or *salade* begins to take on the shape associated with the helmet of heraldry with the helmet having a slit for the eyes, a brim that projected forward and a curved, protruding tail. When worn with a visor, this gave very good protection (figure 250). The schallern was also worn with a *mentionnière*, which was an extension of the breastplate that covered the chin. This appeared around the end of the 15th century. Thus, when the visor was attached, there was all-round protection for the wearer.

A significant advance was made in the design of helmets in Italy around the middle of the 15th century. The *armet* had a hinged lower part and the sides were often attached to the top of the helmet, allowing them to move outwards and upwards (figure 251). Prior to this, helmets were put on over the top of the head, but now donning the helmet became much easier, and it

Figure 249: The bascinet

Figure 250: The schallern

Figure 251: The armet

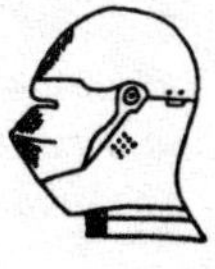

still provided excellent protection. There followed a great number of variations of the armet (which reached England in the early 16th century), and some were decorated extravagantly. Combs appeared, running down the midline of the helmet from brow to neck, and some helmets were fluted and engraved.

Another interesting model was the 15th-century *grid iron helmet*, which was introduced for tournaments. It resembles to some extent the mask of modern fencing, with a bulbous visor made up of a close lattice work of metal. The *grilled helmet* afforded better vision and, in some cases, the lattice was quite open. These forms seem not to have been adopted for use in heraldry.

One helmet that is adopted in achievements is the *tilting helm*, although it is meant to be used only by esquires. It was an all-enclosing helmet that bolted on to the body armour. It must have been immensely uncomfortable (figure 252) and in addition the vision was very restricted. The occularium was merely a thin slit, and the wearer could see only if he leaned forward. It is in this position that it is often depicted by heraldic artists. Later versions of the tilting helm became quite ornate and rather beautiful, and it is often these that feature in achievements.

The use of helmets in achievements is governed by specific rules. An esquire has a wide array of helmets to choose from, but those of higher rank are rather more restricted. The helmet of the monarch is gold and placed affronté (i.e. showing the full face) and has grilles. Royal princes have helmets of silver garnished with gold and peers similarly, with the gold being ap-

Figure 252: The tilting helm

plied to the grilles. A knight or baronet has a helmet of steel that
is set affronté and the visor must be shown open. This means the
armet is most likely to be used by a knight or baronet. The rules
regarding number of bars in a grille (and their colour) tend now
not to be followed, although very specific rules were laid down.
The helmet of the esquire has already been mentioned, although
in Scotland the tilting helm is deemed inappropriate for esquires
and gentlemen, who should have a steel 'pot' helm or helmet. In
the cases of a sovereign or a knight or baronet, the helmet is
placed affronté, while for peers and esquires (and gentlemen) it
is shown in profile. These rules, which were introduced around
1600, enable the rank of the bearer to be determined at a glance.

It is thought by many heraldic authors that the rule regarding
the facing of the helmet results in some difficulties, particularly
when depicting a helmet affronté, which results in an awkward
perspective of the helmet and probably also the associated crest.

CORONETS AND CROWNS

It is appropriate to mention briefly the use of crowns and coronets in heraldry. They are used as an indication of rank, from the
sovereign as head of state, through the royal offspring, dukes,
earls, viscounts, and so on.

The royal crown, that of the sovereign, consists essentially of
a circlet in silver bearing various precious stones (sapphires, emer-
alds, etc). On the rim are set alternately fleurs-de-lis and cross
patées, i.e. crosses that are small at the centre and wide at the

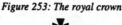

Figure 253: The royal crown

ends (*see* figure 105), in silver and bearing gems. Bridging this part of the crown there are two bands or arches, bearing pearls, that meet at the apex, surmounted by an orb and a cross patée. This is essentially the heraldic form of the crown (figure 253).

Other coronets contain less ornamentation. That of the Prince of Wales contains two rather than four bands of pearls arched over the crown. In other ways it is very similar to the crown of the sovereign. A royal duke or princess has a coronet without the arch of pearls, and grandchildren of a sovereign have strawberry leaves substituted for the two outer cross patées. Around the circlet, an earl's coronet features eight silver balls on long spikes alternating with eight strawberry leaves, while a viscount has sixteen silver balls. A duke's coronet features just eight strawberry leaves, while that of a marquess has four balls on short spikes with four strawberry leaves. Figure 254 shows the general appearance of some coronets of rank.

Figure 254: Coronets of rank. Left to right: duke, marquess, baron, earl

THE CREST

The crest is, of course, the ornament found on the crown of the helmet over the coat of arms. While it is possible to have a coat of arms without a crest, the reverse is not tenable. It seems that the crest may have originated from the practice of painting the primary device of the shield on the front of the helmet and then on the metal protuberance on the top of the helmet.

However, the urge to decorate and show off must have con-

would have been painted and the device associated with a certain person on their shield would have been depicted on the helmet. There are then to be found a number of fan-shaped decorations on helmets that were initially probably designed to provide a more protective role. However, the subsequent decoration of these fans, in the vein of painting mentioned previously, could well have led to the crest that featured the primary charge from the shield itself.

The next stage would be to shape the fan, which would produce a profile, and, if made in thin metal, then it might be sustainable during a battle. Anything more elaborate would probably have been impossible to carry for any length of time. Crests that are now depicted as actual figures would not have been borne in warfare, when the likelier adornment would have been a fan or a plume of feathers. Crests used in tournaments were, of course, worn for only a short time and were made of a light material.

Crests were probably used initially to signify rank and seemed to signify an additional privilege. Their presence seems to have featured quite suddenly at the beginning of the 17th century, when they were granted as a means of confirming coats of arms. While a coat of arms can exist alone, a crest cannot, and invariably from that time a crest was granted with arms when it was proper to do so. When tournaments ceased, the coats of arms became more decorative in nature, and the crests subsequently became less and less sustainable as a realistic adornment to the helmet.

According to some authorities, a little while after their inception crests became hereditary, being passed down through the female line. In Scotland, crests tend to be less important than in England and often are simpler, although sometimes there is little distinction between families.

Crests are now shown upon a coronet, chapeau or wreath. If

two crests feature, they face dexter, and the one on the dexter side is the first. The central one is first if there should be three, but such occurrences are not common. The crests of the four countries, England, Scotland, Wales and Ireland, are:

England: a crown surmounted by a lion statant guardant crowned, or.

Scotland: an imperial crown surmounted by a lion sejant, guardant, displaying a sceptre and sword or.

Wales: a dragon passant guardant gules.

Ireland: an ancient diadem surmounted by an embattled tower, a stag courant rising from the portal.

THE WREATH AND MANTLING

THE WREATH

The wreath is the circular strand resembling a rope that fits onto the top of a helmet at the foot of the crest. It is traditionally shown as having six twists alternately of the principal metal and principal colour of the shield (figure 255), and these are the same as used in the mantling. This is technically called a *wreath of the liveries*. The livery colours are subject to certain regulations, and initially were probably derived from the colours of the cloth and facings of the family's retainers. Then the tinctures were taken from the shield. If the field is part metal and part colour, these constitute the livery colours. However, if the field is partly two colours, the colour mentioned first in the blazon is accompanied by the metal of the major charge. In the absence of a metal, argent should be used. If an ermine is used as

Figure 255: A wreath or torse

the field, then the background of the fur is one livery tincture, thus 'ermine, a bend sable' would give argent and sable.

If any of the regulations cannot be applied, the livery colours are taken as argent and gules. This often happens with animals shown proper.

THE CHAPEAU

The chapeau or *cap of maintenance* (sometimes also the *cap of dignity*) is used in some crests in the place of a wreath. The chapeau consists of a cap of scarlet velvet lined with ermine, which is turned up to form a rim split at the back (figure 256). It is associated with rank and is borne by peers or anyone who has royal blood and seems therefore to be linked with Parliamentary supremacy.

In Scotland the chapeau is associated with the minor barons. It is a privilege of the feudal baronage and showed possession of jurisdiction. The different groups of minor barons are distinguished by using a different colour for the cap. So 'gules doubled ermine' represents barons that previously had their own jurisdiction; 'azure doubled ermine' was for those who were chiefs of baronial houses but who no longer held the baronial fief. The ermine becomes *ermines* (or *contre-ermine*, i.e. white marks on a black field) for certain barons, e.g. old earldoms.

Figure 256: A chapeau

THE MANTLING

The mantling or *lambrequin* is the cloth or cape that is draped from the top of the helmet. It may also have been made of leather. It was probably fastened to the armour at the shoulders and its primary function was protection. It protected the helmet from the burning heat of the sun, which otherwise would have been unbearable. It would also have afforded some protection from the rain, which would very quickly have caused rust to form in the moving parts of the helmet. How much the rusting process would have been slowed is debatable, however.

An additional and probably incidental benefit was that the cloth also aided the wearer in battle, because the sword of an opponent would not strike cleanly if it became entangled in the cloth. The deadening effect of the cloth was thus a boon, but the inevitable result in the life of a battle-hardened individual would be, according to some authorities, that his mantling became somewhat shredded! The plausibility of this explanation can be left to the judgement of the reader. Nevertheless, the outcome in heraldry has been that the mantling is shown in many coats to be composed of several flowing and rather ornate pieces. Some heraldic artists have shown a more realistic representation but many attempts at such artistry satisfy neither style.

The mantling takes its colours from the principal tincture and metal of the shield. It is termed, for example, 'azure doubled argent'. This would be the mantling of someone beneath the rank of peer. Peers have mantling 'doubled ermine', and the sovereign, 'or doubled ermine'.

MOTTOES

The motto is, of course, a short sentence or word, usually depicted on a scroll and placed beneath the shield if in England. In Scotland, the practice differs, and the motto is usually placed above the crest. If there are two mottoes for a Scottish achievement, one is also placed beneath the shield. Also in Scotland, the motto is included with the achievement when it is registered. In an English grant of arms, the motto is not referred to, and it is not hereditary.

Mottoes seem to have appeared in the 1700s; before then there were few, if any. The origin of the motto, according to some authorities, lay in the battle cry or war cry of the family. This may be the case, but few mottoes seem to have the content of a battle cry, and the vast majority of mottoes are hardly appropriate for use in battle to rally the faithful, particularly as a large proportion are in Latin! In Scotland the battle cry may be called the *slogan* or *slughorn*, and it is restricted to the clan chief. Some slughorns are the same as the motto.

Another theory is that the motto is derived from the badge. The badge is not part of an achievement, but it was a distinguishing mark of an individual or family (or clan) that could be displayed on liveries and standards. Badges were used by servants, retainers and dependants as well as the family (*see also* page 114). Many badges have associated words and mottoes, and as the distinction between the crest and the badge became blurred, there was some degree of flexibility, and often the motto from the badge was attached to the crest. It thus seems quite likely that the motto, as also the badge, was not designed for and probably not carried into battle.

There are many peculiar mottoes whose origin can only be speculated upon while others form a pun on the family name or allude to it. Some examples are given below. Because there are different branches of the same family separated geographically, the same motto may be found in different parts of the country, but the converse is also true. Thus people with the same name in different parts of the country may have different mottoes.

Anderson	*Crest*: an oak tree, ppr.; *Motto*: Stand sure
Anderson	*Crest*: a hand holding a pen, ppr.
	Motto: Honesty is the best policy

Ashburnham	*Crest*: out of a ducal coronet, an ash tree ppr.
	Motto: Will God, and I shall
Bell	*Crest*: a human heart between two wings
	Motto: Forward, kind heart
Betenson	*Crest*: a griffin's head couped, ppr.
	Motto: Que sera sera (What will be, will be)
Bryson	*Crest*: a hand holding a horn, ppr.
	Motto: Ever ready
Coats (Cotes)	*Crest*: an anchor, ppr.; *Motto*: Be firm
Cockburn	*Crest*: a cock's head, ppr.
	Motto: I rise with the morning
Corbet	*Crest*: a raven's head erased, sa.
	Motto: Save me, Lord!
Crawford	*Crest*: a phoenix rising out of flames, ppr.
	Motto: God show the right
Dakyns	*Crest*: a dexter arm embowed, ppr., holding a battle-axe ar.
	Motto: Strike, Dakyns, the Devil's in the hempe
Donald	*Crest*: an arm in armour embowed, brandishing a sword, all ppr.
Drummond	*Crest*: a falcon, ppr., armed, jessed and belled, or.
	Motto: Lord, have mercy
Erne (Earl of)	*Crest*: a dragon's head couped, vert, fire issuing from the mouth and ears, ppr.
	Motto: God send grace
Ferguson	*Crest*: an arm in armour, grasping a broken spear, all ppr.; *Motto*: True to the last
Fitzgerald (Bart.)	*Crest*: a boar passant, gu., armed and bristled, or.
	Motto: Shanet a boo
Formby	*Crest*: a dove, ppr.
	Motto: Semper fidelis (Always faithful)
Gardiner	*Crest*: a griffin's head or, gorged with a chaplet of laurel, vert, between two wings expanded, az.
	Motto: Persevere
Grant	*Crest*: a rock, ppr.; *Motto*: Immobile
Heron	*Crest*: a demi-lion ar.; *Motto*: By valour
Home	*Crest*: a lion's head erased, ar., collared gu.
	Motto: True to the end

Kinloch	*Crest*: an eagle soaring aloft; *Motto*: Yet higher
Lang	*Crest*: a dove, in its beak an olive branch, ppr. *Motto*: Mercy is my desire
Lawson	*Crest*: two arms embowed, habited, erm., supporting the sun, ppr.; *Motto*: Rise and shine
Megget	*Crest*: a lock and key, or; *Motto*: Lock sicker
Mercier	*Crest*: a demi-huntsman, winding a horn, ppr. vested az.; *Motto*: Blow shrill
Miller	*Crest*: a lion rampant, sa., between its paws a crossmoline, gu.; *Motto*: Forward
Oliphant	*Crest*: a crescent or; *Motto*: What was may be
Packwood	*Crest*: a demi-lion rampant, ar., holding with his dexter paw, and supporting with his sinister, a bell, sa., with canton erm. *Motto*: None is truly great, but he that is truly good
Pennycoock	*Crest*: a man winding a horn; *Motto*: Free for a blast
Porteous	*Crest*: a dove and olive branch, all ppr. *Motto*: I wait my time
Roche	*Crest*: on a rock ppr., an eagle purp. with wings displayed *Motto*: Mon Dieu est ma roche (God is my rock)
Rose	*Crest*: a harp; *Motto*: Constant and true
Scott	*Crest*: a hand holding a pen *Motto*: Vive la plume (Long live the pen)
Sharpe	*Crest*: a hand holding a dagger in pale, distilling drops of blood; *Motto*: I make sure
Spiers	*Crest*: an arm in armour embowed, wielding a lance, ppr.; *Motto*: Advance
Sutherland	*Crest*: a cat salient, ppr.; *Motto*: Still without fear
Thompson	*Crest*: a lion rampant, gu., ducally gorged or. *Motto*: Go on, and take care
Turnbull	*Crest*: a bull's head cabossed, sa., armed vert. *Motto*: Courage
Urquhart	*Crest*: a boar's head erased, or. *Motto*: Mean, speak and doe well
Wood	*Crest*: a savage from the loins upwards, in his dexter hand a club erect, and wreathed about the temples and loins with laurel, all ppr.; *Motto*: Defend

Young (Bart.)   *Crest*: a demi-unicorn couped, erm., armed, crined
                   and unguled, or, gorged with a naval coronet, az.,
                   supporting an anchor erect, sa.
                   Motto: Be right and persist

This is merely a small selection from the multitude of mottoes
that exist. However, it shows the apparent peculiarity of some
and the puns used in others, where the motto links to the name
or the crest. A number of mottoes occur quite often, such as
Forward, *Suivez raison* ('follow reason') and *Semper paratus*
('always ready').

BADGES

Badges are often referred to as accidental bearings and do not
have any effect on the coat of arms. It seems the heraldic badge
as understood today came into use around the middle of the
14th century, although before then badges of some description
could be found. Badges became important as an indication of
ownership and could be put on property, in addition to being
worn by servants and retainers. Badges were also another opportunity for embellishment and decoration.

The history of badges seems to be rather vague, but apparently
some families with a badge but no crest, on the occasion of a
visitation (*see* page 15), took the opportunity to register their badge
as a crest. The lack of a record for badges in England also means
that origins and derivations are unclear. However, badges were
part of animosities in the past, namely when one group of people, perhaps the retainers of a noble, wore the badge as something more than it was—a symbol of political power. This led
eventually to virtual armies who would be willing to fight for
their overlord. The Wars of the Roses fall into this category.

The lack of regulation pertaining to badges leaves their use
and depiction in heraldry subject to personal choice. When

shown with the achievement, badges will usually be placed on either side of the crest. The badge best known today is probably that of the three ostrich feathers of the Prince of Wales. There are as well the shamrock, thistle and rose of the home countries.

There are many interesting badges, particularly in royal circles. That of Edward IV comprised the white and red roses of York and Lancaster combined, and the Tudor rose of Henry VII was made up of a rose gules bearing a rose argent in its centre, symbolizing an end to the turmoil of the Wars of the Roses. Richard I had a crescent upon which is placed an estoile, and Henry VII had two badges, one a sunburst with the sun's rays emanating from dark cloud, and the other a portcullis, crowned.

Several families used knots of various types, probably the best known being the Stafford knot, which was used quite improperly and taken up by many. It became the 'Staffordshire' knot, so its origin as the badge of the Lords Stafford was obscured.

In Scotland the badge is often regarded as the same as the chief's crest. There it was shown within a belt and buckle with the motto. The badge could be inherited with the feudal fief and was worn by all concerned, while the leader displayed his arms and banner.

HERALDIC SUPPORTERS

Supporters are animals, birds, beasts or human figures that are placed on either side of the shield and look as if they are holding it up. The origin of supporters is, as with many other aspects of heraldry, open to debate. It seems the likeliest explanation for them is that they were added to the sides of a shield on a seal and took the form of a badge or an animal.

It is a very rare occurrence to see a single supporter; they invariably are shown in pairs. Certainly in some old Scottish patents, when supporters were called *bearers*, just one is shown, and, although a few examples survive, it is not commonplace.

The rules governing supporters differ quite markedly between Scotland and England. In England, the right to bear supporters is limited almost exclusively to peers and a number of orders of knighthood, and special dispensation is required to award them to others. In many instances it is hereditary while for others it is limited to the person receiving the grant. The feudal system of Scotland rendered the situation different. There, supporters can be granted to all Scottish peers and British peers with Scottish coats of arms (or who receive a Scottish title). Even then, the supporters must be registered in the Lyon Register before they may be used. The right to use supporters also falls to others, including many lairds and the heirs of minor barons, clan chiefs, long-established families and some knights. In addition, the Lord Lyon, who has complete control of matters heraldic in Scotland, has the authority to grant supporters when he thinks it appropriate. However, this right is rarely exercised.

Probably the greatest range of supporters is to be found among the animals. The lion is again one of the animals to feature most commonly, and it is usually shown rampant and either guardant or regardant. Tigers also feature quite prominently, as does the griffin. Goats and rams of various styles are seen, and both the horse and Pegasus occur, often in the arms of peers. Other mythical animals in this context include the dragon, cockatrice and wyvern (*see* pages 84–90), the latter commonly depicted standing on one claw, holding the shield with the other claw.

The human figure is also used extensively as a supporter, and quite often is represented as a savage. Equally popular is a man in armour. Birds may feature quite strongly in number, but in variety there are few. It is not surprising to learn that the eagle is almost the sole representative.

The science of heraldry, whether in its proper form or not, has spread worldwide, and the use of supporters is exemplified admirably in the crests of a number of countries. Figures 257 to 260 show some of the variety of supporters that may be found.

Figures 257–260: Examples of supporters

FLAGS

Heraldic flags come in several forms, each of a different size and shape. They include the banner, standard and pennon.

BANNER

The banner is usually a square flag that displays the arms as found on the shield. The crest, supporters and motto do not appear on the banner. The early forms of banner were rectangular, the width often being about half the height. The banner is the main flag of a knight, and no one below the rank of knight banneret (i.e. a knight who is entitled to have a square banner carried before him into battle and at tournaments; *see* page 125) is entitled to it. There were particular sizes to be adopted for the banner, depending again on rank, as shown below:

the sovereign—5 feet square (1.52 metres square)

princes or dukes—4 feet square (1.22 metres square)

earls—3 feet 6 inches square (1 metre square)

baronets and feudal barons and noblemen of lesser rank—3 feet square (91 centimetres square)

A rectangular banner is the correct way of displaying arms on a house flag where the occupant has the right to bear arms. The size of a house flag depends on the height of the building but 5 x 4 feet (1.52 x 1.22 metres) are considered the correct proportions. The size of banners in Scotland has been stipulated by the Lord Lyon as:

peers—5 x 4 feet (1.52 x 1.22 metres)
feudal barons—3 feet 9 inches x 3 feet (1.24 x 0.91 metres)
other chiefs—3 feet 6 inches x 3 feet 3 inches (1 x 0.99 metres)
chieftains—3 feet x 2 feet 6 inches (91 x 76 centimetres)

STANDARD

The standard is a long, rectangular flag that seems to have been used first in the 14th century. It tapered at one end, where it was often split into two tails. The standard was used in battle and was probably a rallying point for the retainers. The field of the standard would be divided per fess into the owner's tinctures. Starting at the staff, the standard would carry the cross of St Andrew or St George (depending on nationality) so that everyone could see immediately the origin of the bearer. Then the remainder would bear the owner's tinctures and upon this field would be placed the main charges, the badge (or badges semé) and then the motto, the latter probably positioned bendwise. The whole thing would be edged with a fringe or bordure compony.

The royal standard as used in a tournament or encampment would have measured 30 feet (9.14 metres) in length and 9 feet (2.75 metres) in width. When it was used in the field, the length of the standard indicated rank. A duke would have a standard about 21 feet (6.4 metres) in length, a marquess 19 feet (5.8 metres), a viscount 16 feet (4.8 metres), a peer 15 feet (4.6 metres), a baronet 13 feet (4 metres), and a knight 12 feet (3.6 metres).

The use of standards seems not to have lasted for a very long time, although their presence persisted a little longer in the case of funerals.

PENNON

The pennon is a small variety of flag that is essentially triangular and elongated in shape, with either a split 'swallow-tail' end or a slightly blunt point. It carried the owner's arms, badge or other heraldic item, and was fastened to a lance. There is reference to a smaller version of the pennon, which was called the *penoncel* or *pencil* (figure 261).

Figure 261: The general shape of a pennon

In Scottish heraldry, there is also a *guidon*, which is about two-thirds the length of a standard and upon which is displayed the badge or crest. Pennons are then about half the size of guidons. The motto on a guidon is positioned lengthways, into the tail of the flag.

Also referred to in Scottish heraldry is the *pinsel*. This is also a triangular flag, measuring approximately 4 feet 6 inches (1.6 metres) in length and 2 feet (60 centimetres) in height. It contained the crest, buckle and motto with a coronet or cap. It was used by chiefs or chieftain barons or, in their absence, by their representative commander. This seems very similar to the small version of the pennon (especially if referred to as a pencil).

THE UNION JACK

Perhaps the commonest flag of all, the Union Jack was first gen-erated in the reign of James VI and I. It was then the flag for the united kingdom that was formed from Scotland and England and comprised the cross of St George (arg., a cross gu.) with the cross of St Andrew (az., a saltire arg.) (figure 262). The field ar-gent of St George's cross is indicated by the fimbriation (edg-ing) around the margins of the cross.

The cross of St Patrick (arg., saltire gu.) was included on the Union with Ireland in 1800. The heralds designing the flag gave equal weight to the two saltires, producing a 'saltire, party per saltire quarterly, arg. and gu.' all on a field az. Those parts of the saltire blazoned gu. were then fimbriated arg., and the red cross of St George with a thin fimbriation arg. was then placed over the top to create the current Union Jack. The Scottish national flag is thought to have been introduced by Angus II, king of the Picts. This flag can be hoisted by any Scotsman (or worn as a badge), as applies to St George's and St Patrick's crosses and the Red Dragon of England, Ireland and Wales respectively.

The origin of the name Union Jack for the flag of the Union has been subject to some debate. The derivation of Union is ob-vious, Jack is less so. One theory suggested it originated from Jacques, the French form of the name of James VI and I, in whose reign the first flag of union was created. This seems un-likely as later versions do not adhere to this practice. Another

Figure 262: The first Union Jack

Figure 263: The Union Jack

possibility is that the word *jaque*, which in French refers to a garment upon which heraldic emblems were depicted, may have been transposed to flags. *Jaque* would obviously have been easily anglicized to 'jack'.

BLAZONING AND ITS RULES

As mentioned in an earlier section, 'to blazon' is to describe in words a particular coat of arms. This is done in accordance with the rules of the science of heraldry such that it is impossible for it to be misunderstood and so that anyone who has sufficient knowledge can reconstruct the coat of arms. 'To emblazon' is, of course, to show a coat of arms in colour. There are relatively few rules of blazoning, and they are described below:

1 The starting point is to mention if the shield is quartered or impaled. Impaled is when two coats of arms are conjoined (joined together) on one shield, palewise (figure 264). Quarters have already been mentioned (*see* figure 30), and a shield is quartered to indicate descent from an heiress, amongst other things. Each quarter or side of the shield is blazoned by the rules as if it were a shield. One would state that it is dexter or sinister (in the shield conjoined palewise) and the number of the quarter stated. Often the first and fourth quarters are the

Figure 264: Coats conjoined palewise

same, in which case the blazon would commence 'Quarterly first and fourth . . . .'

2 The field is then described by its division, if there is one, and then by its tincture. If it is a simple field, there would be just the word for the colour. If it is a composite field, the division should be stated, e.g. 'party per fess arg. and az.'. The word 'party' is used in English heraldry (and is actually often omitted), but in Scotland the term is 'parted'. Where there is more than one tincture, that mentioned first is the one in dexter or in chief. In a field quarterly, the first and fourth quarters are described before the second and third.

3 Next in the list is the principal charge or ordinary. Where it is an ordinary, it is termed 'arg., a chevron az.', for example. If there is also a charge in addition to the ordinary, it might be 'az. a chevron between three mullets arg.'. If the colour of the ordinary and charge is the same, it is put at the end of the description. If they differ, then both must be stated, e.g. 'az. a chevron arg. between three mullets, or'. If an ordinary is subjected to a particular line of partition (*see* page 25) then this must be stated, e.g. 'az. a pale arg. engrailed'.

4 When charges automatically fall into a specific position with respect to the ordinary, then no details need be mentioned. Clearly, three figures around a chevron can only be placed two in chief and one in base. Similarly, a fess would have two above, one below, while a bend between two charges has one on either side. The same principle applies to four charges and a cross.

  However, if the disposition of a charge or charges with respect to an ordinary is not obvious, it must be stated, thus a bend with one charge, a chevron with four, a cross with one charge, and so on. One might have 'az. a chevron arg. between three mullets in chief and one in base, or'.

5 Next are named any other charges on the field in order of importance. They should be specified by means of their position and tincture. Charges on the ordinary are next described, again stating position, outline and whether colour or metal.

6 If there is no ordinary on the shield, then the principal charge is mentioned first. If no position is specified, it is understood to occupy the centre of the field. If it does not, then its position must be stated, with its colour or metal. Subsidiary charges follow, likewise with position, where required, and tincture, and then charges on charges, all in a logical sequence.

7 When an ordinary surmounts a charge (i.e. it is placed on top), the charge underneath is described first. The ordinary on top is said to debruise the charge underneath.

There are several additional points of guidance that may be mentioned for the student of blazoning. It has been stated previously (*see* page 25) but is worth saying again that, in using tinctures, a colour may not be placed on another colour, nor a metal upon a metal. If the field is a metal, it can take only a colour or a fur, but there are exceptions, as discussed previously.

It is a general point of procedure that the same number should not be repeated, nor should the same tincture. In all cases the minimum number of words should be used. Thus to avoid naming the same tincture more than once, a blazon will use 'of the first', 'of the second', 'of the last', etc, when referring to subsequent use of the same tincture. Examples might be:

—'a dexter arm embowed, vested ar., cuffed sa., in the hand, ppr., a sword, of the first, hilt and pommel or', and

—'a demi-Moor, ppr., habited gu., rimmed round the collar with two bars or, tied round the waist with a ribbon ar., wreathed about the head of the last and second, in his dexter hand a gem-ring, of the third'.

All animals should be described, with the position specified, whether passant, statant, rampant, and so on. An ordinary or subordinary is usually mentioned before any other charge, although there are some exceptions (canton, chief, bordure, quarter). Other rules and points of guidance will be found in those sections that consider the ordinaries and related topics.

Finally in this section, the arrangement of multiples of a charge is considered, because additional points of blazon are covered. Two charges—let us use an annulet—may be placed vertically in pale (figure 265) or horizontally in chief, base or fess. Figure 266 shows them in fess. When three are used, unless an ordinary dictates the position, they are placed two over one (figure 267). If one were placed uppermost, it would be called one over two. Three annulets could also be placed in fess, chief base, pale or in bend (diagonally). Four would most likely be positioned two over two in a square configuration that is of-

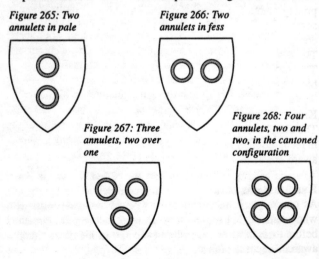

Figure 265: Two annulets in pale

Figure 266: Two annulets in fess

Figure 267: Three annulets, two over one

Figure 268: Four annulets, two and two, in the cantoned configuration

ten called *cantoned* (figure 268). Five arranged as found on a die would form a saltire, termed thus: 'five annulets; two, one, two, in saltire'. The format of six can obviously vary from three rows of two (six annulets: two, two, two) to a pyramid or its inverse (three, two, one). In all cases, the blazon commences with the figures at the top of the shield, or in chief.

KNIGHTS AND TOURNAMENTS

ORDERS OF KNIGHTHOOD

The title of knight was conferred upon someone for services performed in a campaign. As the number of individuals with a particular order of knighthood grew, they formed into something akin to a society under the control of the sovereign. A surprising number of orders have developed over time, although some are now 'extinct'. Some of the better-known examples are considered briefly below. The titles are somewhat abbreviated. The full title is somewhat longer. For example, Knights of the Thistle are actually Knights of the Most Ancient and Most Noble Order of the Thistle.

KNIGHTS BACHELOR

The oldest order in England, which initially was conferred only in recognition of services in war. It was, and remains, a personal award and cannot be passed down the family.

KNIGHTS BANNERET

As one might deduce, this order evolved from those knights who had the right to have a square banner (*see* page 117) carried before them in battle or at tournaments. It was a military order, awarded because of some brave act in the field of conflict. The knight would be presented to the sovereign or general; the end of his pennon would be cut off to render it square, and it was then fastened to the top of the lance. Such knights were certainly created late in the 13th century, and possibly before, but it is now an extinct order.

KNIGHTS OF THE GARTER

This is the oldest and most honourable order in Europe and was founded in 1344 by Edward III, and the reigning monarch is the sovereign of the order. St George is the patron saint of the order, and Windsor Castle is its college. Of course, the garter is the main emblem. It is made of gold-edged blue velvet upon which is embroidered the motto, *Honi soit qui mal y pense*, which means 'dishonoured be he who thinks ill of it'. The order comprises 25 knights, the sovereign and royal princes.

In the heraldic version, a representation of the garter encircles the shield. A knight of this order is also permitted to add to his coat a collar gold, the collar of the order. In reality this consisted of a gold collar weighing 30 troy ounces, which is just over 13 ounces (93 grams). (Troy weight is used specifically for weighing gold and silver.) The collar contains 26 enamelled buckled garters, and in the centre of each is a rose. The garters are joined by knots of gold. Attached to the collar is an enamelled gold pendant of George attacking the dragon.

KNIGHTS OF THE THISTLE

This order was reinstated by James II and VII in 1687 and subsequently incorporated by Queen Anne in 1703. It consists of the sovereign and 16 knights (or brethren) who have the motto *Nemo me impune pacessit*, 'no one provokes me with impunity', which is the motto of the kings of Scotland. Knights in this order may surround their arms with a green circle edged in gold, which bears the motto in gold letters. The badge or jewel of the order is St Andrew supporting a cross.

KNIGHTS OF ST PATRICK

This is, of course, an Irish order. It was founded in 1783 by
George III, and the order incudes 22 knights in addition to the
monarch and royal princes. The arms are surrounded by a plain
sky-blue circle edged with gold with the motto *Quis Separabit,
MDCCLXXXIII*, 'who will divide, 1788'. The collar of the order
is gold with alternate roses and harps joined with gold knots.
The roses are enamelled alternately white leaves within red and
vice versa, and an imperial crown over a harp of gold is in the
centre of the collar.

The star or jewel is 'argent, a saltire gules surmounted with a
trefoil vert, charged with three imperial crowns or', the whole
enclosed in a circle of gold bearing the motto.

KNIGHTS BARONET

An hereditary honour created in 1619 by King James II and VII,
apparently to encourage members of the English gentry to settle
in Ulster. The arms of a knight baronet can be distinguished by
the augmentation of a human hand gules upon an escutcheon
that is carried either in the centre or chief of the shield.

KNIGHTS BARONET OF NOVA SCOTIA

This order was instigated in 1625 by King James VI and I with
the intention of encouraging capitalists to settle in this province.
It was short-lived, ending in 1707, but was hereditary. The arms

*Figure 269: The badge for the order of knighthood
for knights baronet of Nova Scotia*

are borne on either an escutcheon or a canton and are 'argent, St Andrew's cross azure, overall an escutcheon or, with a lion rampant gules within a double tressure of the same, ensigned by a royal crown' (figure 269).

KNIGHTS OF THE ORDER OF THE STAR OF INDIA

This order was initiated in 1861 during the reign of Queen Victoria. It was awarded to eminent people in India and those who gave outstanding service to what was then the British Empire. It has three classes: Knights Grand Commanders, Knights Commanders and Companions, the first of which has the circlet of the order surrounding their shield. The circlet is light blue and bears the motto 'Heaven's light our guide'. Surrounding this is the collar, consisting of Indian lotus flowers alternating with palm branches and the rose of England (red and white). The Imperial crown sits in the centre of the collar and from it hangs the badge, which includes an onyx cameo of Queen Victoria.

KNIGHTS OF THE ORDER OF THE INDIAN EMPIRE

This order also has three classes, as for the Star of India. The Knights Grand Commanders and Knights Commanders have the circlet around their shield. The circlet is purple, upon which is the motto *Imperatricis auspiciis*, 'empress commander', in gold letters. The collar is used only by the Knights Grand Commanders and comprises lotus flowers, elephants, peacocks and Indian roses, with an Imperial crown in the centre, all linked by golden chains. This order was begun in 1877 to celebrate the establishment of Queen Victoria as Empress of India.

KNIGHTS OF THE BATH

This is a long-established and very honourable order. It was a military order of knighthood established in 1399 by Henry IV. He created 46 such knights at his coronation. The order then fell into abeyance but was revived in 1725 by George I, and the number of knights created rests with the sovereign. There was just one class in the order and recipients were denoted by the letters KB. They had circlets of crimson edged with gold around their shield, and the motto was *Tria juncta in uno*, 'three joined in one'.

After the Peninsular Campaign, the Prince Regent, later to become George IV, restructured the order. By 1815 there were many officers who were deemed meritorious of such an award, and so the order was increased in scope to include three classes. The first class, and the highest, is the Knight Grand Cross (abbreviated to GCB), and this honour is bestowed upon very senior military personnel, such as major generals. The next class is Knight Commander (KCB), which applies to those above the rank of captain and colonel in the navy and army respectively. Companions of the Order (CBs) form the third class. In 1847, a civil equivalent of this order was established.

OTHER ORDERS OF KNIGHTHOOD

The order of *St Michael and St George* was established in 1818 and is bestowed upon those who have distinguished themselves in foreign affairs. It also has three classes, the Knights Grand Cross having a circlet, collar and badge. The Knights Commanders have circlet and badge, while Companions have just the badge. The collar has lions of England alternating with Maltese crosses and an Imperial crown over two lions passant guardant, each holding seven arrows. Two similar lions occur on the opposite side of the collar. The motto on the circlet is *Auspicium melioris aevi* ('an omen of a better time').

The *Royal Victorian Order*, which was instituted in 1896, is unusual in that it has five classes. There is no collar with the order, and the circlet is a dark blue with the motto 'Victoria' in gold.

The order of *Knights of the British Empire* was started in 1917.

Knights Grand Cross, Knights Commanders and Knights Bachelor of the various orders use in their arms the helmet in the open affronté position. Companions have the closed helmet in profile.

TOURNAMENTS

Tournaments were essentially war games in which knights fought for honour and reputation in a public exhibition of combat. Tournaments occurred in peacetime and were an opportunity to train the nobility in the use of arms and techniques of battle. In fact, tournaments were commonplace in France in the 11th century, and the practice was brought to Britain with the Normans. Their history has been somewhat chequered, however, and on many occasions the event became very rough, with the audience participating, particularly if they felt their representative had been dealt with unfairly. Indeed, Henry II did not allow any tournaments to occur, although a modified form was reintroduced by Richard I.

By the 1400s, tougher rules and better armour meant there were many fewer casualties, and tournaments were generally much better organized. Medieval events of this nature were an opportunity for grand ceremony and display, and of course armorial bearings would be shown to the full by the heralds. Often, invitations would be sent to suitable candidates far and wide, even abroad, and the knights would usually arrive about four days before the start. They would bring with them all their trappings, including shields, banners, surcoats, horse with full regalia, and the esquires who would carry the lances and pennons.

The knight would make challenges in person, and a number would be engaged in one tournament. For these purposes, the lances were made of wood with no iron tip, and swords would almost certainly have neither edge nor point. Two groups of knights would enter and ride around the enclosure, paying their respects possibly to the sovereign but certainly to the assembled lords and ladies. They would then take up their positions and, upon the charge being sounded, rush headlong towards each other. The contest could last several hours. Those who became unsaddled withdrew, the victory depending on the number who fell.

In addition to the battle-like tournaments, there were also jousts, which were duels. It seems there were several forms of joust, including *sharp lance running*, in which the object was to knock your opponent from his horse using a lance. The *free joust* could be fought anywhere, and the spear had a special attachment that allowed an opponent's armour to be held without being penetrated. Another form of joust was the *tilt*, in which there was a wooden barrier (called a tilt) about 5 feet (1.5 metres) high between the contestants. Participants charged, with the barrier on their left side, and attempted to unseat their opponent. The armour for tilting was very heavy (perhaps as much as 100 pounds or 45 kilograms), and it was heavier on the left side, which is where the opponent's lance would impact. The horses involved would not work up too much pace because, with the knight's armour and the animal's own protection, they could be carrying around 350 pounds (160 kilograms) of armour.

The spear or lance used in tilting would probably have been made of fir, perhaps 15 feet (4.5 metres) long and 3 or 4 inches (7 or 10 centimetres) in diameter. This would have added another 30 pounds (13.6 kilograms) or so to the poor horse's burden. The lance was placed in a rest (called the *queue*), which was fastened to the armour. When a lance was broken on an opponent, it had to be dropped immediately to avoid further injury.

Another variation was the *tourney* or *mêlée*, a team event in which the weapons were usually made of wood. Despite all the rules and precautions that eventually were introduced, it is not surprising that in what was literally a mêlée, there were usually many injuries, possibly some fatalities and a good number of wounded. Many knights and personages of higher rank have met with their end at such events. In 1559, Henry II of France was accidentally killed in a tournament because a splintered lance entered his visor. This resulted in a ban in France, but the tradition continued in England until the early 1600s.

CADENCY

Cadency is the part of heraldry that enables a distinction to be made between brothers of the same family and the families of brothers. These distinctions are accomplished by means of marks on the shield. These marks are called *differences*. The Scottish system has a number of distinctions from that in England, primarily in the use of bordures, and these are considered on page 135.

The first *mark of difference* to find use seems to have been the *label*, which was and is used to indicate the eldest son (*see also* page 56). After the label, the *bordure* can be traced back to the 14th century as a mark in cadency. However, it tended to signify merely that the bearer was not the head of the household, and in modern usage in England it is retained only because of historical precedent.

In many cases, in the early days of this subject, a change in arms was the outward manifestation of a difference. If a younger member of a household became the head of a different house or the lord of an estate, whether by marriage or other means, it became necessary for him to have a distinct coat of arms. The likelihood is that in many cases, new or very changed arms were taken up. The main ways in which coats of arms were altered include the addition of a charge to an ordinary or to the field; the change of a tincture; the addition of a canton, quarter or label; altering lines of partition, and so on. Later, there developed a proper system utilizing the label, bordure and bend, and then eventually the more recent means of identification.

There are certain rules worth mentioning before the marks of difference are itemized. During the lifetime of his father, the eldest son would modify his arms with a label of three points, couped (i.e. cut off square) at the ends, that was placed at the centre chief position of the shield. The tincture used could be decided by the bearer, but it can follow the rules of tincture, i.e. by avoiding putting like on like (e.g. colour on colour). However, because these marks should not be mistaken for charges, to put them as colour on colour, or metal on metal, may make blazoning easier. Usually argent/white was not selected. The label argent is used only by royalty as a cadency mark. When the father dies, the eldest son takes the undifferenced shield. The children of the son, while the grandfather lives, show marks of difference upon the label, reverting to a difference upon the original arms when their father becomes head of the house. It is necessary to ensure that the label is placed correctly, e.g. if the father's shield is quartered then the label must debruise all the quarterings. Likewise, if the son succeeds to the mother's arms, the label must not cross the quartering of this part of the shield, only the father's. The marks of difference are:

eldest son	a label
second son	a crescent
third son	a mullet
fourth son	a martlet
fifth son	an annulet
sixth son	a fleur-de-lis
seventh son	a rose
eighth son	a cross moline
ninth son	a double quatrefoil

Figure 270: The marks of cadency

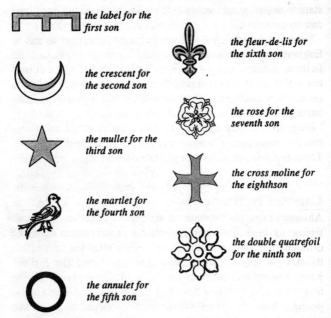

the label for the
first son

the crescent for
the second son

the mullet for the
third son

the martlet for
the fourth son

the annulet for
the fifth son

the fleur-de-lis for
the sixth son

the rose for the
seventh son

the cross moline for
the eighthson

the double quatrefoil
for the ninth son

Figure 270 illustrates these marks, which are also used to distinguish the families of different brothers, called the second house, third house, and so on. The presence of a label without another charge and not placed on another mark is an indication of the heir apparent of a family.

The result of this is that the sons of the eldest son have a label upon which are placed the marks listed above. In the second house the marks feature on a crescent. Thus the third son of each of five sons in a family would have a mullet charged on a label, crescent, mullet, martlet and annulet respectively. The system works reasonably well, but inevitably there are circumstances within a succession that lead to ambiguities, but these can be overcome.

There are no marks of difference for women, thus sisters in England (and Ireland) are not distinguished from one another. In these circumstances, a daughter carries the cadency marks of her father (if there are any) but upon marriage it may be removed if, when her arms are marshalled with those of her husband, there is sufficient distinction.

Illegitimate children do not carry marks of cadency, and a special procedure has to be undertaken to enable them to bear arms. There is a mark of difference to indicate bastardy.

CADENCY IN SCOTLAND

Although there are elements of the system in Scotland that are similar to those in England (e.g. in the use of certain marks of difference), it is essentially quite different. The head of the family and the male heir are allowed to take arms, but for any younger sons the regulations are quite different. In effect, the Scottish system is purer than that used in England because the younger sons (called *cadets*) are obliged to 'matriculate' the arms in their own name in the Lyon Office. The differences applied are thus decided by the official office of heraldry in Scotland, which leads to a consistency not seen in England. This is called a 'right to rematriculation' rather than a 'right to bear arms'. Once the correct difference has been obtained, the arms may be used.

The system involves each son receiving a bordure of a different colour, or sometimes a charge from his mother's coat of arms. Then younger sons of younger sons have additional differences whereby the bordure may be defined by a different line of partition or the bordure may be parted (i.e. divided) per bend, per pale, per gyronny, and so on. The orders in which the bordure colour and lines are applied are as follows:

Bordure colour	Lines
or	engrailed
argent	invected
gules	indented
azure	embattled
sable	wavy
vert	nebuly
purpure	rayonée
tenné	raguly
ermine	nowy*
contre-ermine	contre-nowy
erminois	dovetailed
pean	potenty
vair	urdy‡
potent	round embattled

* nowy is a line with a single, short arch or hump in it.

‡ urdy or urdée is a line of partition that resembles nebuly but is composed of angular lines (figure 271).

Figure 271: The line of partition urdy

The tincture rules do not apply strictly to bordures, but if a metal shield (say argent) were due to receive a bordure argent, then it would likely be represented as a bordure chequy or counter-compony.

In Scottish heraldry, the illegitimate son is given full rights.
Providing full proof of paternity is produced, he can matriculate
like anyone else.

BASTARDY

Although not part of the subject of cadency, bastardy is effec-
tively a form of differencing. In the early days of heraldry, the
public perception of bastardy was very different from what it
later became. At that time, illegitimacy mattered little, and bastard sons tended to follow their own wishes when establishing
their heraldic connections.

The main reason that any differences were developed in this
matter was the need of families to establish the true heirs. Thus
the arms of a bastard were marked to show he was not entitled
to the family estates. However, it was conceded that such a person belonged to the family even if he was not in the line of succession.

As such, the differences employed initially were numerous
and diverse. The earliest differences seem to have been the bend
followed by the bordure. The bend would be placed over the
shield and usually in the sinister form, but the existence of a
bend (dexter) was an indication that it was merely a mark of difference and in no way a 'black mark'. Much the same situation
applied to the bordure, in that there was no clear usage of this as
a mark of illegitimacy.

The bend sinister was superseded by the bendlet or riband sinister in this case, and when such a charge debruises a coat, it is
clear that it is a bastardized version. The bendlet sinister has
emerged as a mark in the guise of a baton sinister (*see* figure
46), which, if depicted in a metal, is an indication of illegitimacy of a member of royalty on the male side. It should be
noted that in relation to bastardy, *marks of distinction* are used
in preference to marks of difference.

Since about the end of the 18th century, the bordure wavy (*see* figure 138) has been used as an indication of illegitimacy in England, while in Scotland it is the bordure compony (*see* figure 146). The crest in English arms may also be marked with a bendlet sinister wavy or a pallet wavy.

For an illegitimate son to bear arms, he must petition for a patent of arms to the appropriate king of arms (*see* page 16), and if suitably qualified he will be given a patent of arms. These may be new arms, totally unconnected with those of his father, in which case there would be no need for marks of distinction. A second route to gaining arms is to petition the sovereign for a royal licence to bear arms (and the father's name). If this is granted as a result of the paternity being recognized, the College of Arms determines the marks of distinction for the arms and crest. In Scotland, such matters rest entirely with the Lord Lyon.

MARSHALLING COATS OF ARMS

Marshalling is the practice by which upon one shield are shown two or more coats of arms joined together, representing marriage, alliance and descent, over several generations. This may be achieved by several methods, one of the earliest being quartering.

QUARTERING

This is the practice by which a husband quartered the arms of his wife, or his wife's female ancestor should this be the source of the land. After marriage with an heiress, the arms of the man are placed in quarters 1 and 4, and the woman's in quarters 2 and 3 (*see* figure 30). This is the simplest case.

If in a later generation another quartering is introduced, it occupies quarter 4. Further additions, say to five, begin to introduce complications. In this case, the first quarter can be repeated and the six quarters arranged in two rows of three, or in an upper row of three and a lower row of two. The placing of these and subsequent quarterings on the shield has to follow set rules so that the pedigree is properly stated. There is, however, some scope, in that the first quartering may be repeated and, when numerous, the quarters can be put into any number of rows to fit the shield best. All the quarterings from the father are arranged sequentially, and then in the same sequence are arranged the arms and quarterings from the mother's side. Thus the first quartering is the *pronominal coat* (the strict male line of descent) and the second the coat of the first heiress who married into the family.

In Scotland, quartering is to all intents and purposes not permitted unless the bearer rematriculates. The arrangement of the quarterings is then determined by the office of the Lord Lyon. The Scottish shield has just four quarters. If more have to be shown, then *grand quartering* is adopted, i.e. one or more of the quarters is itself quartered. It seems that, in practice, quartering is adopted primarily for heiresses of considerable importance. In addition, quartering may result from the terms of an heir of entail, i.e. a person acquiring property as a result of a particular remainder in a deed of entail. By this method quarterings are found for states, feudal lordships, and so on, and not just personal heiresses. In Scotland the heir of entail is called *heir of tailzie*.

DIMIDIATION

This is a method of marshalling that is no longer used, if only because of the confusion it caused with the conjoining of some coats. In this practice, half the man's shield was taken and melded onto the opposite half of the wife's shield. Where the two heraldic designs were quite different, this would have been entirely acceptable. In some instances, and certainly in the case of two shields with the same ordinary, however, the end result was a shield that looked like one simple coat rather than the combination of two coats. Initially this problem was overcome by including about two-thirds of each shield in its own half, but it was soon realized that it was quite feasible to put the whole shield into the half available. In so doing, this created another method of marshalling, *impalement*.

Depending on the lineage of the woman, the marshalling of arms will differ. If the woman is not an heiress in heraldic terms, hers and her husband's coats are impaled. If the wife is an heir or coheir, the arms are not conjoined by impalement but by *superimposition* (*see* page 142). This latter case is where the arms of the wife's family are placed upon an inescutcheon that is laid over the top and in the centre of her husband's arms. The inescutcheon is called an *escutcheon of pretence*, because her husband 'pretends' to her family's representation. In heraldic terms, an ordinary husband and wife are called *baron* and *femme*. Further, a woman is defined as being an heir or heiress if she is an only child, if all her brothers die without leaving any off-spring, or she may become an heiress 'in her issue', by dying and leaving offspring who survive the offspring of her brothers (i.e. the latter become extinct). The word 'coheir' is used when there is more than one daughter in such cases.

IMPALEMENT

This is when the arms of a husband and wife are placed on the same shield, divided vertically down the centre. Because the line occupies the position of the ordinary called the pale, it is termed 'parted per pale'. The coat of arms of the man is placed on the dexter side of the shield and that of the woman on the sinister side (e.g. figure 272).

Figure 272: Arms impaled, with the man's on the dexter side

Second marriages can be shown on the one shield, although it is probably less cumbersome and clearer to place two shields side by side. However, if a man so wishes he can place the arms of his second wife on the shield, in which case the sinister side would be divided per fess, with the first wife's arms being placed in sinister chief and the second wife's occupying sinister base. Alternatively, the husband's arms may be placed in the centre with the first wife on the dexter and the second on the sinister. Similar arrangements can be applied to three and four wives in the unlikely event of this occurring.

There are certain modifications to the method of impalement depending on the rank of the individuals concerned. If the wife is an heiress, her arms are placed on an escutcheon, as in *superimposition* (*see* page 142). If the husband is a knight (of any order) he bears two shields because the decorations of knighthood cannot be applied to his wife's arms. The dexter shield then carries his own arms with the appropriate insignia and encircling collar, and the sinister shield carries the impaled arms of husband and wife, all surrounded by a wreath of laurel. Companions of an order of knighthood hang their badge beneath the shield, and the arms of the wife can either be impaled or placed upon an escutcheon of pretence. A Knight Grand Cross would be able to add supporters, if appropriate, which would be placed outside both shields.

In the case of a peer, the arms are impaled as for a commoner, and the wife's arms are thus placed beneath the coronet, helmet, supporters, etc, of her husband. However, if the peer is also a knight, then they revert to the use of two shields.

Conversely, if the wife is a peeress, it is not permissible for the husband to take on her rank. Thus, if she marries a commoner, her arms are placed upon an escutcheon of pretence, with the coronet above. However, the supporters appropriate to her shield cannot be added to the shield of her husband. The wife's arms are then repeated to the side, upon a lozenge. In this case the husband's shield is again placed on the dexter side. The coronet of rank is placed above the lozenge and the supporters also feature.

SUPERIMPOSITION

The practice of superimposition has already been referred to as resulting in an *escutcheon of pretence*, where an heiress has her arms featuring on an inescutcheon placed centrally over the arms of her husband. In essence, this means that the husband pretends to represent his wife's family. However, when she dies, the representation clearly passes, in reality, to her son and heir.

The escutcheon of pretence is not used by the children of a marriage whose parents have that shield. The children carry the arms of their parents in quarterly fashion, thus passing them on to succeeding generations. The practice of placing the arms of an heiress upon an inescutcheon is not used in Scottish heraldry.

The general procedure in Scottish practice is that the arms are conjoined, as in impalement. If either coat of arms has a bordure, that part of it next to the palar line is left out, a relic of dimidiation.

FUNERAL HATCHMENTS

The use of funeral hatchments or escutcheons was something of a passing phase in heraldry, although it persisted for perhaps a couple of hundred years in practice. The hatchment is essentially a lozenge shape within which is the coat of arms of a deceased person. It was a wooden frame and the arms were painted on it, whereupon it was hung at the main entrance to the home. The coat of arms is shown impaled if appropriate.

The difference between the normal coat of arms and the hatchment is that the background of the lozenge, upon which the coat of arms was painted, was black. The black was put behind the part of the shield that referred to the deceased; therefore, if a man died leaving a widow, the dexter part of the background was black. The remaining part of the shield, behind the widow's arms, would thus remain white. If the woman died, the colourings would be reversed. If a widower died, then all the background would be black.

AUGMENTATIONS AND ABATEMENTS

An *augmentation of honour* is a prized addition to any coat of arms. It is given by the sovereign to mark a particularly distinguished act and it becomes hereditary. Augmentation may be granted as escutcheons, cantons, quarterings or chiefs. Crests have also been granted as augmentations of honour, but in general this method of reward and recognition is used rarely.

Abatements of honour are in effect the opposite of augmentations. It is held by some in the field of heraldry (although others would argue vehemently against) that abatements were charges placed upon a shield to indicate that the bearer had done something to cause offence or had contradicted the standards of the day. The subject is a little controversial because many believe that abatements were actually an invention of the 17th century. There is much to be said for the argument that considers abatements to be contrary to the spirit and structure of heraldry, and in any event, how could anyone be made to carry a 'negative' charge against his will? Equally, one could argue that a temporary abatement could be charged until a good deed justified its removal. Although there seem to be few if any examples of abatements, this is not surprising, because of their temporary nature and because, obviously, no one would wish his misdeeds to be catalogued for future generations.

In favour of the existence of abatements, it seems that some of the ancient authorities on heraldry do record details of them. This being so, it can be said that, when adopted, abatements used particular tinctures and ordinaries that would rarely have been seen otherwise in Britain. The tinctures used were tenné and sanguine (*see* page 22), and the ordinaries included the point and the gore.

The *point* cuts off a corner of the shield with a line at 90 degrees to the line that bisects the angle (figure 273) and, unless specified otherwise, it is a base point. The *gore* is two concave lines originating from the middle base and sinister chief points, meeting at the fess point (figure 274). Other variations included the *escutcheon reversed* (an inescutcheon upside down) and the *delf*, a small square placed centrally on the shield. These devices would have been used to signify lying, boasting, seduction, revoking a challenge, drunkenness, and so on. One cannot help but think that if abatements were used to denote such acts as lying, just about every coat of arms would have been festooned with points!

Figure 273: The point dexter abatement of honour

Figure 274: The gore sinister abatement of honour

FAMILY CRESTS

From all the foregoing, it can be seen that the basics of heraldry are essentially quite straightforward, and very quickly it becomes possible to blazon a simple achievement. With practice, the more complex aspects can also be mastered and the vast treasure store of heraldry can be opened.

Below are the descriptions of crests of a reasonable number of family names, which may prove interesting. The same name is commonly found spread geographically throughout the English counties and the other countries of the Union, but more often than not, the arms are quite different. It may be, therefore, that the particular details described here do not match someone's known crest, but both are valid nonetheless. The crests are from old sources, and in some cases it will be noticed that the entry is incomplete or contrary to some rules of blazoning, but, even so, the crest can be deciphered quite readily.

Abbot	a snail ppr.; out of a ducal coronet, a horse's head; a demi-unicorn, erm., armed and maned, ar. (gorged with a collar az.), studded or
Abercrombie	a cross crosslet, fitched, gu.
Abraham	the sun or
Adam	on a mount vert, a sword and a cross crosslet in saltire, ppr., banded gu.
Adams	out of a ducal coronet or, a demi-lion affronté, ppr.; a griffin's head gu., between two wings or
Agnew	an eagle rising regardant, holding in the dexter claw a sword, all ppr.; the sun shining on the stump of a tree, ppr.
Ainsley	a pelican's head erased, ppr.; an arm embowed, grasping a scimitar, ppr.
Ainsworth	a falcon, wings expanded and inverted, ppr.

Alcock	a demi-swan, erm., wings expanded, issuing out of a ducal coronet az.; a cock, erm., beaked, membered, crested and wattled, or
Alderson	from behind a mount vert, with a branch of alder thereon, the sun rising ppr.
Alexander	a horse's head ar., bridled sa.; an arm in armour embowed, holding a sword, ppr.; a hand holding a pair of scales, equally poised, ppr.
Allan	an eagle rising ppr.; a demi-lion rampant ar., ducally crowned gu., holding in the dexter paw a cross-potent or, and in the sinister a rudder gu.
Allen	a talbot passant or, collared gu.; out of a ducal coronet or, a horse's head ar.; a hound statant sa., on a mount vert; a dexter hand issuing out of flame, holding up a human heart
Allison	a peacock ppr.
Allot	a cubit arm erect, vested or, cuffed ar., holding in the hand, ppr., a mullet or
Anderson	a crescent or; an oak tree ppr.; a ship in full sail ppr.; out of a ducal coronet ar., a hind's head or, pierced through the neck with an arrow sa., feathered ar.
Andrew(s)	a stag's head erased sa., attired or; a moor's head in profile, sa.
Appleby	an apple or, stalked and leaved vert
Archer	a bull's head erased, gu.; a quiver; a dexter hand and a sinister arm, issuing from the wreath, drawing an arrow in a bow to the head, ppr.
Armstrong	an arm in armour, grasping a sword, az., hilted and pommeled or
Arnold	a dolphin embowed ar.
Arrowsmith	seven arrows ppr., enfiled with a ducal coronet or
Arthur	a pelican sa., in a nest or, vulnerating herself, gu.
Ashley	a plume of feathers ppr.; on a chapeau gu., turned up erm., a plume of five ostrich feathers ar., issuing out of a ducal coronet or
Asken	an ass ppr.; an arm ppr., holding a sword ar., hilted or, enfiled with a Saracen's head couped, ppr., wreathed or and sa., blood issuing, gu.

Aspinall	a demi-griffin erased, sa., beaked, legged and collared, or
Ashton	a bull's head, couped, or, armed sa.; a chapeau gu., turned up erm., on each side thereof, within the ermine, a horn ppr.
Atherton	a hawk ppr., legged and beaked or
Atkins	an etoile; two greyhound's heads addorsed, collar dove-tailed, per pale or and az., counterchanged, erased gu.
Atkinson	a pheon or; a demi-eagle, wings displayed or, collared sa.
Austin	a lion's paw erased, ppr.; a three-quarter spread eagle, with three annulets on the breast
Bacon	a boar passant, erm., armed and hoofed or
Baggeley	a ram's head az., attired or
Bailey	a demi-lady, holding in her dexter hand a tower, in her sinister a laurel branch, vert
Baird	an eagle's head erased, ppr.; a ship in full sail, ppr.; a cockatrice, wings indorsed, gu.
Baker	a naked dexter arm holding up a purse.; a tower ar., be-tween two laurel-branches ppr.; a rose tree vert, flow-ered or
Baldwin	a squirrel sejant, or; a lion rampant, az., holding a cross crosslet fitchée, or
Balfour	a crescent or; a palm tree ppr.; a hand in armour holding a truncheon, ppr.
Ball	a turtle dove ppr.; out of a ducal coronet, an arm in mail, embowed, holding a fireball, all ppr.
Banks	a dragon's head erased, ar.
Barber	out of a ducal coronet gu., a bull's head ar.
Barclay	a sword in pale, ar., hilt and pomel or; a cross pattée, gu.
Barker	a bear's head, sa., muzzled or; a bear sejant, or, collared sa.
Barlow	an eagle's head erased, ppr., in the beak an escallop shell
Barnard	a demi-bear rampant, sa., muzzled or
Barnes	in rushes, ppr., a duck ar.; an etoile pierced, or; a falcon, wings expanded, ar., ducally gorged, beaked and leg-ged, or
Barton	an acorn or, leaved ppr.; an owl ppr.

Bates	a demi-lion rampant, but holding in the dexter paw a thistle, and in the sinister, a fleur-de-lis, all ppr.
Beaumont	on a chapeau az., semée of fleurs-de-lis, turned up, erm., a lion passant, or
Bell	a hawk's bell stringed, ppr.; a bell or; a human heart between two wings
Berry	between the horns of a crescent or, a cross pattée gu.; a griffin's head erased, per pale, indented ar. and gu.
Bird	a martlet ppr.; on a dolphin ppr., an eagle or, wings expanded
Bishop	out of a mural coronet ar., a griffin's head sa., beaked or
Black	an arm in armour embowed, ppr., wielding in the hand, also ppr., a scimitar ar.
Blair	a boar's head couped, ppr.; a dove, wings expanded, ppr.
Blundell	a squirrel sejant, ppr., collared, cracking a nut, or
Blythe	an arm embowed, ppr., habited per pale or and az., holding a battle-axe, of the last, headed ar.
Bond	a demi-pegasus az., semée of etoiles or
Booth	a lion passant, ar.; a boar's head, erased and erect, sa., armed or, in the mouth a spear head, ar.
Bowen	a hand rising from a cloud in fess, holding a sphere
Bowes	a sheaf of arrows, or, bound in a girdle az., and surmounted with a motto
Bowles	a buck's head ar., attired or; a demi-boar az., armed, hoofed and bristled, or, pierced through the chest with an arrow of the second, headed ar.
Bowyer	a tower triple-towered, gu., thereon a semi-dragon; a falcon rising, ppr., belled or
Brady	a cherub ppr.
Brett	a griffin's head between two wings, az., beaked or
Bridges	on a tower ar., masoned sa., a dove rising, ppr.
Brooke	on a chapeau, a wing displayed, gu., charged with a chevron ar., and thereon a lion rampant, sa., crowned or
Brown	a griffin's head erased, or; a hand holding an open book, ppr.; a dolphin naiant, ppr.
Browne	a beehive with bees volant, ppr.; an eagle displayed, with two heads, sa.

Bruce	the sun rising from a cloud, ppr.; an eagle's head couped, ppr.
Burnet	a vine branch slipped, ppr.
Burton	on a ducal coronet or, a wyvern vert; a gauntlet ppr.
Butler	a dexter arm in armoury, gauntleted, az., garnished or, holding a sword, sa., hilted of the second
Caldwell	a cock's head, winged sa., crested gu., in the beak a cross patée fitched, or
Cameron	an armed arm, grasping a sword, ppr.
Campbell	a boar's head erased, or
Carpenter	a demi-lion rampant, gu., ducally crowned or, collared sa.; a stag's head ar.
Castle	a tower in flames, ppr.
Cavendish	a serpent nowed, vert
Chadwick	a martlet ar.
Chambers	a lion's head sa., langued gu.; within a mountain vert, a man working in a copper mine holding a pickaxe elevated, ppr., his cap, shirt, drawers and hose ar., shoes sa., the planet Venus rising behind the mountain, or
Chapman	out of a crescent, per pale or and gu., a unicorn's head of the last, maned, horned and guttée of the first; a fleur-de-lis or, between two olive branches, vert
Christie	a phoenix's head in flames, ppr.
Churchill	out of a ducal coronet or, a demi-lion rampant, ar.
Clark	in a gem ring or, set with a diamond sa., a pheon ar.
Clarke	a cross formée, or, between two wings displayed, az.; a demi-lion rampant, or, holding a cross crosslet fitched, az.
Cockburn	a cock's head ppr.; a dexter arm holding a broken spear in bend, ppr.
Cole	a bull's head couped, sa.; a demi-dragon, holding an arrow, or, headed and feathered ar.
Collins	on a chapeau gu., turned up erm., a griffin statant, per pale ar. and gu.
Colquhoun	a laurel branch slipped, ppr.
Colvil(le)	a hind's head ar., charged with a cross patée, sa.
Cook	a demi-lion gu., in the dexter paw an etoile or

Cooke	a wolf's head ar., ducally gorged gu.; an ostrich, in its beak a horseshoe
Cooper	a demi-leopard guardant, holding a rose, all ppr.; a dove with an olive branch, ppr.
Crawford	a hand holding a lancet, ppr.; an increscent, chequy ar. and az.; a phoenix rising out of flames, ppr.
Cunningham	on a ducal coronet or, a mount vert, thereon a stork statant, in its mouth a snake, the tail coiled, its body ppr.; an oak tree ppr.
Curtis	a lion sejant, ppr., in the dexter foot a shield
Dalziell	a dexter hand brandishing a scimitar, all ppr.
Darling	a female ppr., habited in a loose robe ar., the body pink, and flowing round her a robe az., holding in the dexter hand a cross crosslet fitched, gu., and in the sinister a book, ppr.
Davies	a fawn couchant, ppr.; a lion's paw erased, holding a mullet of five points
Davis	a wolf passant, erm.
Dawson	an etoile of six points, or
Dixon	a sphere ar., charged with a pale, indented vert; a stag's head erased, per pale dancetté sa. and or, attired counterchanged
Donaldson	on a rock az., a raven sa.; a cock crowing, ppr., within two adders in orle
Douglas	a human heart gu, winged and crowned or, charged with a crescent chequy, gu. and ar.; a martlet sa.
Drake	a ship under ruff, drawn round a globe with a cable rope, by a hand out of clouds, all ppr.; a reindeer's head couped, ar.
Draper	a stag's head erased, gu., gorged with a fess between two gemelles, ar., and charged with a fleur-de-lis sa.
Duff	a hand holding an escallop; a demi-lion gu., in his dexter paw a broad sword, ppr., hilt and pommel or
Dunn	on the point of a sword in pale, a garland of laurel, ppr.; two swords in saltire, ppr., entwined with a ribbon az., thereto a key pendant, sa.
Eden	an arm embowed, habited barry of four az. and gu., holding in the hand, ppr., a bunch of wheat, vert

Edgar	a demi-ostrich rising, in the beak a horseshoe
Edmonds	between two wings indorsed, a lion couchant guardant, all or
Edwards	an antelope rampant, sa., bezantée, attired or; a unicorn sa., double-horned or; on a mount vert, a horse's head erased, or, charged on the neck with a chevron gu., between two oak branches, ppr.
Egerton	three arrows ar., headed and feathered sa., banded or; a lion sejant, gu., supporting in the dexter paw a battle-axe ar., staff of the first, and in the sinister a laurel branch, ppr.
Elliot(t)	a demi-sea horse, az., finned or; a dexter hand ppr., holding a crescent, sa.
Ellis	in a crescent gu., an escallop or; a mermaid with a mirror and comb, ppr.
English	a rose branch ppr., flowered gu.
Evans	an eagle's head between two wings, sa., in the beak a rose gu., stalked and leaved, ppr.; a lamb passant, holding a banner
Ewing	an arm in armour, couped and tied at the shoulder, embowed, resting the elbow on a chapeau gu., and holding a sceptre
Fairfax	a lion's head erased, sa., gorged with three bars gemelle and ducally crowned or
Farmer	a cock's head gu., combed and wattled or, in the beak a rose, of the first, stalked and leaved, vert
Farquhar	a dexter hand couped, ppr.
Ferguson	issuing from a cloud, a dexter hand grasping a broken spear in bend, ppr.
Finch	a griffin passant, sa.
Fisher	a demi-seadog rampant, or; an anchor, cabled, ppr.
Fleming	a hand in armour, gauntleted, holding a sword, ppr.
Fletcher	a pheon, point upward, per pale erm. and sa.; a dexter arm in armour embowed, holding an arrow in fess, all ppr.
Forster	a dexter arm in armour, embowed, ar., purfled and braced or, round the arm a sash vert, in the hand ppr., an arrow of the third, broken off at the head, barbed of the second

Foster	a stag trippant, ppr.; a lion's head erased, or, collared gu.
Fowler	a stork ar., membered gu., holding in its bill a cross formée fitched, or; on a chapeau, an owl rising guardant, ppr.
Francis	an eagle displayed, erm., beaked and membered or
Fraser	a demi-eagle in flames, ppr.; a stag's head erased, or, armed ar.
Freeman	a demi-lion rampant, gu., holding between its paws a lozenge, pierced, or
Frost	an old man's head, ppr.
Fryer	a heraldic antelope's head erased, per fess ar. and gu., gorged with a ducal coronet or, attired of the second
Gale	a unicorn's head, paly of six or and az., attired of the first; a greyhound's head erased, bendy-wavy of six, or and sa.
Gardiner	a griffin's head erased, az., charged with three bends or; out of a mural coronet or, a dexter arm in armour embowed, sa., garnished of the first, holding a pennon gu., charged with a pomegranate or, staff ppr., headed gold
Gardner	an elephant's head, erm., eared sa., armed or; a griffin's head erased, ppr., charged with a crescent or
Geddes	on a mural coronet, a bundle of seven arrows, banded or
George	a hawk rising, ppr.; a demi-talbot sa., collared, indented and eared, or, between two fir branches vert
Gibbs	an arm in armour embowed, ppr., gauntleted or, holding in the gauntlet a poleaxe ar.
Gilbert	issuing out of rays or, an eagle's head ppr.
Giles	a demi-chevalier, holding a sword
Gillespie	an anchor ppr.
Glover	a fleur-de-lis or, between two wings sa.
Godfrey	a pelican's head erased, or, vulning, gu.
Goldsmith	a stork sa., bezantée or
Goodman	the battlement and upper part of a tower ar., thereon a woman couped at the knees, habited az., hair dishevelled or, in her dexter hand a rose gu., stalked and leaved vert
Gordon	a buck's head at gaze, ppr., attired and ducally gorged or; a dove and olive branch, ppr.; a hart's head couped, ppr., charged with a crescent ar.

Gould	a demi-lion rampant, or, holding a scroll, ar.
Gower	a demi-eagle or
Graham	issuing out of a cloud, a hand reaching to a garland, all ppr.; an eagle devouring a crane
Grant	a burning hill ppr.; an oak tree ppr.
Gray	a scaling ladder, of two rows, in bend, ppr.; on a ducal coronet or, a phoenix in flames, ppr.
Green	a buck's head erased, erm., attired or; a rose gu., barbed vert, seeded or, environed by two laurel branches, ppr.
Grey	on a mount vert, a bear or; a unicorn erect, erm., armed, crested and unguled, or, behind it a full sun, ppr.
Griffith	a lion rampant, sa.; a woman's head affrontée, ppr.
Grosset	four arrows, points downwards, and a strung bow in saltire, all ppr.
Gunn	on a chapeau az., a fox sejant, or
Hall	a talbot's head sa., spotted or; on a chapeau gu., turned up ar., a greyhound sejant, erm.
Hamilton	a hand holding a heart, ppr.; a cubit arm erect, holding a scimitar, ppr.
Harding	a mitre gu., banded and stringed, or, charged with a chevron, ar., fimbriated or, and thereon three escallops, sa.
Harley	out of a castle, triple-towered, ar., a demi-lion rampant, gu.
Harris	a buck's head, chequy ar. and az., attired or; a hedgehog, ppr., charged with a key, az.
Harrison	a demi-lion ar., holding a branch, vert
Hart	a sundial or, on a pedestal gu.; a lion's head couped, erm., ducally crowned or
Harvey	a leopard ar., ducally gorged and lined, or; a lion passant, ppr., holding a trefoil, vert
Hawes	a goat's head sa., in its mouth a holly branch, vert
Hawkins	a demi-moor, manacled, ppr.
Hay	the sun in his splendour; a demi-arm holding aloft an ox yoke, ppr.
Henderson	under a tree, a boar passant; a hand holding a mullet, surmounted by a crescent
Herbert	a wyvern with wings indorsed, vert, in his mouth a sinister hand couped, gu.

Hill	a buck's head, per pale gu. and az., the nose or, collared of the last; on the trunk of a tree lying fesswise, or, a falcon, ppr., beaked and belled of the first
Holland	a sinister wing, or
Holmes	a demi-griffin; a lion's head erased, in the mouth a sword
Hooper	a boar's head erased at the neck, az., bezantée, armed and crined, or
How(e)	on a chapeau, ppr., a martlet sa.
Howard	on a chapeau gu., turned up erm., a demi-hind salient, ppr., charged with a cross fleury fitched, ar.
Hughes	a lion couchant guardant, or; a lion rampant, or, holding a thistle slipped, ppr.
Hunter	a fir tree, ppr.; a hunting horn vert, stringed gu.; two hands shooting an arrow out of a bow, all ppr.
Hutchinson	a cockatrice, wings expanded, az., combed, wattled and membered, or
Hutton	a man ppr., wreathed round the temples and loins, vert, in his hand three leaves, of the last
Hyde	a unicorn's head, gorged with a collar compony
Inglis	a demi-lion holding a mullet
Innes	a boar's head erased, sa.; two hands joined fesswise, holding a sword, all ppr.
Ironside	a dexter hand, in fess, couped, holding a sword in pale, surmounted by a laurel crown, all ppr.
Irvine	a sword and a palm branch in saltire
Jackson	a horse at full speed, ar., gutée de sang; a hand ppr., holding a boar's head, erased and erect, sa.
James	a demi-lion rampant, erminois, holding an escallop gu.; out of a ducal coronet or, a demi-swan ar.
Jenkins	a battle-axe, handle or, head ppr.
Jennings	a demi-dragon, erminois, wings indorsed, gu., erased of the last, holding a battle-axe, erect, az.
Johnson	a dexter arm in armour, embowed, firing a pistol, all ppr.; a stalk of wheat, ppr.; a wolf passant, in its mouth a sprig of woodbine in full blossom, all ppr.
Jones	a demi-lion rampant, or, between its paws a mullet gu.; on a chapeau gu., turned up erm., a stag ar., attired vert

Kay	a goldfinch, ppr.
Keith	a demi-lion rampant, ppr.
Kemp	on a garb, or, a pelican, vulning herself, ppr.
Kendall	a hand holding a sheaf of arrows, points downwards, all ppr.
Kennedy	a dolphin naiant, ppr.; on a rock, a goose, ppr.
Kerr	a chevalier in full armour, holding a horse by the head, ppr.; the sun, ppr.
King	a lion passant, ermine, ducally crowned, or; a demi-griffin, or
Knight	between two wings, gu., a spur, leathered, or; a friar, vested ppr., having in his dexter hand a cinquefoil slipped, ar., in the sinister a cross pendant from the wrist, the breast charged with a rose, gu.
Knowles	a parrot, feeding on a branch bearing cherries, ppr.
Lake	a sea horse's head and neck, couped, ar.
Lamb	a lamb, ar.; a demi-lion rampant, erminois, in the dexter paw a mullet, vert
Lambert	a sphinx passant guardant, or, face ppr., under the dexter foot a rose, gu., seeded and leaved, vert; on a mount, vert, a centaur passant regardant, the human parts ppr., the other erm., girt about the loins with a garland of laurel, of the first, drawing a bow and arrow, gu.
Lancaster	a hand brandishing a sabre, ppr.
Lane	two eagles' heads addorsed, issuing from a crescent, or, the dexter, gu., the sinister, az.; a dexter arm, habited ermines, turned up and indented ar., in the hand, ppr., a mullet, az.
Lang	a tower, ar., masoned, sa.
Langley	a dexter gauntlet in fess, holding a sword in pale, all pr., the blade enfiled with a dragon's head, sa., couped at the neck, gu.; between two sprigs of laurel, vert, a pheon, or
Latham	an eagle, wings elevated, erminois, preying on a child, ppr., swaddled, ar. and az., exposed on a rock of the second
Law	a dove and olive branch, all ppr.; a unicorn's head, ppr.
Lawrence	a demi-turbot, ar., tail upwards.; a griffin sejant, wings indorsed, in the dexter paw a garland of laurel, ppr.

Lawson	a hind's head erased, ar., on the neck three pellets, one and two collared vert; a demi-lion rampant, between the forepaws a mullet of six points
Leake	a cannon, mounted on a carriage, all ppr.
Lee	a leopard passant, bezantée; a falcon or, wings close, gu., preying on an eagle's leg, lying fesswise
Leigh	a cockatrice az., combed and wattled gu.; a greyhound's head ar., between two roses gu., slipped and leaved ppr.
Leslie	a demi-griffin ppr., in the claws a buckle or; a camel's head erased, or, bridled, lined, ringed and gorged with a ducal coronet
Lewis	a horse's head, bridled, ppr.; on a chapeau gu., turned up erm., a greyhound sa., collared or; a lion rampant, gu.
Lindsay	an ostrich's head erased, ppr., in the beak a horseshoe or, about its neck a label of three points, ar.
Lister	a stag's head erased, per fess ppr. and or, attired of the last
Lloyd	a hart trippant, ar., attired or; a demi-lion rampant, ar., issuing from a five-leaved coronet or
Long	a lion's head sa., guttée ar., issuing from a crescent or; on a mount vert, a greyhound courant, sa., collared and lined, erm.
Lonsdale	a bull passant, gu.
Lorimer	a horse courant, ar.
Love	a hand holding an annulet, ppr.
Lowe	a demi-griffin segreant, or
Lucas	an arm embowed, vested sa., bezantée, cuffed ar., in the hand, ppr., a cross crosslet, gu.; an urn ar., flammant gu.
Lyon	a hand holding a sword, ppr., enfiled with a boar's head erased, or
Macdonald	in a bush, a lion's head and forepaws, sa.; a raven sa., standing on a rock az.
MacGregor	an arm in armour, ppr., wielding a scimitar az., hilt and pomel or
MacKenzie	a mountain in flames; the sun in his splendour
Maitland	in the sea, a rock ppr.; a demi-monk, habited grey, in his dexter hand a crucifix, in his sinister a rosary, ppr.
Major	a greyhound rampant, sa., collared ar., on the collar three mullets, of the first

Mallory	a horse's head couped, per pale gu. and az., ducally gorged or
Mansfield	a griffin's head erased
Marshall	a lion passant guardant, or; a chevalier in armour, holding in his dexter hand a marshall's baton, resting on his side, ppr.
Martin	a martin sa., in its beak a buckle ar.; a tower, triple-towered, chequy or and az.; a wood martin ppr., collared ar.
Mason	a tower ppr., masoned sa.; a demi-lion rampant, ar., in its dexter paw a crescent or
Maxwell	an eagle rising, sa., beaked and membered gu.; a stag rising from a holly bush, ppr.
Meredith	a dragon passant, gu., langued az.
Middleton	between two wings erect, ar., a garb or; on a tower az., a lion rampant, gu.
Miller	a demi-lion az., holding between the paws a mascle or; a wolf's head erased, az., collared erm.; a cross moline, sa.
Mills	a wing, barry of ten ar. and vert
Milne	a dexter hand holding a folding book, ppr.
Mitchell	a wheatsheaf vert; a phoenix, rising out of flames, ppr.
Montgomery	a merman ppr., holding a target or; an eagle rising
Moore	a moor's head in profile, ppr., wreathed or and sa.
More	as for Moore; a demi-lion rampant guardant, az., supporting a wheatsheaf vert, banded gu.
Morgan	a reindeer's head caboshed, or; a savage's head affrontée, wreathed.
Morris	a tower in flames, ppr.; a lion rampant, or, charged on the shoulder with a cross couped, gu., within a chain in the form of an arch, gold
Mortimer	a buck's head erased, quarterly or and gu.
Munro	an eagle close, ppr.
Murray	a branch of laurel erect, vert; a horse ar., furnished gu.; a telescope on a stand, or
Napier	a dexter hand holding an eagle's leg erased, in bend, ppr., armed gu.; a dexter hand erect, holding a crescent ar.
Nelson	a dexter arm in armour, couped and erect, ppr., holding a fleur-de-lis, counterchanged
Newton	a bear's head couped ar., muzzled gu.

Nicholas	a lion passant, az., semée of etoiles or
Nicholson	a greyhound's head ar., between two roses gu., slipped and leaved vert
Noble	a demi-greyhound ar., pierced in the breast with an arrow, ppr.
Norton	a tiger's head erased, in the mouth a broken spear or; a maiden's head ppr., garlanded vert
Ogilvy	a sword in bend, ppr.; a sunflower ppr.
Oliphant	a hand pointing to the clouds, ppr.
Oliver	a martlet ar., in its beak a sprig, vert
Osborne	a heraldic tiger statant, ar., crested and tufted sa.
Owen	a demi-dragon gu., winged or; an anchor sa., on the base thereof a lion statant, gu.
Page	a demi-griffin erm., beaked and legged, gu.
Palmer	a wyvern's head or, collared gu., wings expanded, vert, fretty and semée of trefoils slipped, ar.
Parker	a horse's head couped, per pale indented ar. and az.; on a chapeau az., turned up erm., a greyhound or; a talbot's head ar., collared pean, eared gu.
Parsons	a garb of quatrefoils, vert, banded ar.
Partridge	a partridge rising, with an ear of wheat in its beak, all ppr.
Payne	a demi-ostrich, wings indorsed, ar., in the beak a key, or; among grass, ppr., an otter passant, or
Pearce	a cross crosslet fitched, or, issuing from a mural coronet gu.
Pearson	a cubit arm erect, holding a wreath of laurel, ppr.
Perkins	a lion passant, sa., holding a fleur-de-lis gu.
Perry	a stag's head, ppr., pierced through the neck with an arrow or, feathered ar., headed sa.
Peters	between two laurel branches, vert, a boar's head erased, ar.
Phillips	a lion sejant, sa., collared and lined or; out of a ducal coronet or, an arm in armour embowed, the hand, ppr., holding a broken spear of the last, powdered with fleurs-de-lis or
Pickering	a lion's gamb erect and erased, az.
Piper	a magpie sa.
Poole	a unicorn passant, az., tufted, maned and armed or, ducally gorged ar.

Pope	a griffin passant, ppr., collared gu.
Porter	a portcullis ar., chained or; a demi-antelope or, spotted, collared and attired gu.
Powell	a boar passant, sa., collared and lined or; a lion rampant, ar.
Pratt	a demi-unicorn salient, or, holding a mascle az.
Preston	on a tower or, a falcon, wings expanded and elevated, ppr., beaked, legged and belled of the first; an angel, ppr.
Price	a lion rampant, or, holding a rose gu., stalked and leaved vert; a holy lamb passant, bearing a banner charged with a cross
Pringle	a man's heart ppr., winged or
Pritchard	an arm ppr., holding a battle-axe, handle gu.
Proctor	on a mount vert, a greyhound sejant, ar., spotted brown, collared or
Proud	a cross formée fitched, or, charged with five pellets, a chaplet of laurel entwined round the cross, vert
Quin	an arm in armour embowed, holding a sword, ppr.
Radcliffe	in a mural coronet ar., a bull's head sa., armed and crined or
Ramsay	a unicorn's head couped ar., armed or, within two laurel branches in orle, ppr.
Randall	a demi-griffin gu., winged or; an antelope's head couped, or, charged on the breast with four mullets, and in the mouth a rose gu.
Raymond	out of a mural coronet, a demi-eagle displayed, erm., beaked sa., charged on the breast with three ogresses, two and one; on a mount vert, a leopard sejant, per fess or and sa., spotted counterchanged
Read	a falcon with wings expanded, ppr., belled or, statant on a reed lying fesswise, vert
Reeves	out of a ducal coronet, a griffin's head
Reid	a lion passant, tail extended, ppr.; a dexter hand issuing from a cloud, holding an open book, ppr.
Reynolds	a cat couchant, ppr., collared and lined or; a fox's head erased, sa., gorged with a collar, or, charged with three torteaux, on the neck a martlet

Richardson	out of a mural coronet or, a demi-lion rampant, gu., holding between the paws a guidon ar., charged with a slip of oak, ppr., fructed of the first, the staff and tassels of the last; a lion rampant, holding between the fore-paws two oak slips fructed, ppr.
Richmond	a tilting spear ar., headed or, broken in three parts, one piece erect, the other two in saltire, enfiled with a ducal coronet of the last
Rider	out of a mural coronet, per pale or and az., a snake erect, ppr., holding in its mouth a trefoil slipped, vert
Ridley	a greyhound courant, ar., collared or
Riley	a dragon's head erased, sa., charged with a plate and two bezants
Roberts	an antelope's head erased, per fess or and gu.; a demi-lion az., holding a mullet ar., pierced sa.
Robertson	a savage's arm erect and erased, ppr.; a sleeping dog
Robinson	on a mural coronet, chequy ar. and az., a stag's head caboshed, ppr.; issuing from a cloud, a dexter arm erect, holding up a garb.; a buck or, pelletée
Roche	on a rock ppr., an eagle purp., with wings displayed
Rogers	a man's head in armour, side-faced, ppr., helmet or, feathers ar.; a cubit arm in coat of mail, holding in the hand, ppr., a banner, staff and flag, or
Rose	a rose, slipped and leaved, ppr.; a pheasant, in its beak a rose, slipped and leaved, ppr.
Ross	a rose tree bearing roses, all ppr.; a water bouget, sa.
Rowley	an etoile of eight points, pierced
Rudd	a lion rampant, or, holding an escutcheon, az., charged with a canton, or
Rush	a wolf's head erased, erm.
Russell	a demi-lion rampant, ar., holding a cross crosslet fitched, sa.; a demi-lion or, charged with a cross pattée, az., in the mouth an oak branch, ppr., fructed gold, holding between the paws an escutcheon, az., charged with a fess, erminois, between three fleurs-de-lis in chief, and a cross pattée in base, or, from the escutcheon a scroll bearing a motto
Rutherford	a martlet sa.

Ryan	a griffin segreant, az., holding a sword erect, ppr.
Sadler	a tilting spear in pale, or, charged in the middle with an escutcheon, gu.
Salisbury	two lions rampant combatant, ar., ducally crowned or, supporting a crescent of the last
Saunders	an elephant's head erased, sa., eared ar.
Scott	in pales, a dexter arm, vested az., cuffed ar., in the hand a roll of paper, ppr.; a hand holding a pen; a hand holding a book, shut, ppr.
Selby	a saracen's head, couped at the shoulder, ppr., wreathed round the temples, tied in a knot behind, or and sa.
Seton	a crescent gu.; a dragon vert, spouting fire, ppr., wings elevated and charged with a star or
Seymour	on each side of a chapeau gu., turned up erm., a wing or; out of flames, ppr., a phoenix issuant, or
Sharp	an eagle's head erased, az., ducally gorged or, in the mouth a pheon, ar.
Sharpe	a hand holding a dagger in pale, distilling drops of blood
Shaw	a hind's head, quarterly ar. and or, pierced through the neck with an arrow, headed az., the feather broken and dropping, ar.; a hand, ppr., holding a covered cup, ar.
Shepherd	on a mount vert, a stag lodged regardant, ar., vulned on the shoulder, gu.
Sherman	a sea-lion sejant, per pale or and ar., guttée de poix, finned of the first
Shields	a dexter hand gu.; an escutcheon ar.
Shirley	a saracen's head in profile, couped, ppr., wreathed about the head, or and az.
Short	a griffin's head or, in the beak a trefoil, slipped, vert
Sibbald	a cross moline, gu.; two laurel branches in orle, ppr.
Simpson	a cross raguly, suspended thereon an escutcheon, per bend sinister, charged with a lion rampant; a snake nowed in a knot, vert
Sinclair	from clouds, ppr., an etoile rising, ar.; a polecat ar.; a cross engrailed, sa.
Skinner	a griffin's head erased, ar., in the mouth a dexter hand couped at the wrist, gu.

Smart	a hawk's head between two wings, ar., holding in the beak a thistle, ppr.
Smith	a heron's head erased, in the beak a fish, ppr.; a saltire gu., surmounted of a fleur-de-lis, ar.; a demi-unicorn gu., maned, horned, unguled and tufted, ar., holding a lozenge or; an elephant's head couped, or
Smyth	on a chapeau gu., turned up erm., two wings az., billet-tée or, on each a bend, erm.
Somerset	out of a naval coronet or, a hippocampus, erect, ar.
Spencer	on the trunk of a tree lying fesswise, raguly, and at the dexter end a branch erect, vert, a talbot sejant, gu., eared or, collared or; a moorhen, ppr.
Stafford	on a ducal coronet, per pale sa. and gu., a swan rising, ar., beaked sa.
Standish	an owl ar., beaked and legged or, statant on a rat, sa.
Stanley	on a chapeau gu., turned up erm., a cradle or, containing a child swaddled, gu., thereon eagle preying, of the third; a griffin's head, erased
Stapleton	a saracen's head in profile, ppr.
Starkey	a stork's head erased per pale ar. and sa., in the beak a snake, vert
Stephen	on a rock ppr., a salmon lying fesswise, ar., in its mouth a rose gu., stalked and leaved vert; a cock gu.
Stevens	a garb or, banded; a demi-falcon displayed, or
Stevenson	a garb erminois.; a dexter hand issuing out of a cloud, holding a laurel garland, all ppr.
Stewart	a bee volant, ppr.; a holly leaf slipped, vert; a pelican ar., winged or, feeding her young, ppr., in a nest, vert
Stirling	an eagle displayed, in the dexter claw a sword, and in the sinister a pistol, ppr.; a ship under sail ppr.
Stone	on a mount vert, a horse courant, sa., bridled, crined and hoofed or; a demi-cockatrice rising, ar., winged and crested or
Strachan	a ship in full sail ppr.
Strang	two hands clasped, ppr., couped at the wrists
Stuart	a pelican feeding her young, all ppr.; a bird standing on a wheatsheaf, or
Sutherland	a cat sejant, sa.

Sutton	a lion's head erased, per pale ar. and vert, collared gu.; three annulets interwoven, or
Swift	a pegasus in full speed, vert, wings indorsed, or
Symonds	a vine fructed, ppr.; a dolphin embowed, ppr., finned or
Tait	a horse's head couped, ppr.
Taylor	a demi-greyhound az., collared, in the dexter paw an annulet or; a lion's head erased, erm., collared gu., thereon three roses ar.
Temple	a talbot sejant, sa., collared and ringed or
Thatcher	a seax ppr.
Thomas	between two spears erect, or, a Cornish chough, ppr.; three arrows, two in saltire and one in pale, ppr., banded gu.
Thompson	an arm in armour embowed, quarterly or and az., in the gauntlet, ppr., a broken lance, of the first
Thomson	a dexter hand couped, in fess, ppr., holding a cross crosslet fitched, az.; a crane, in its beak a palm branch, all ppr.
Thornton	issuing from the summit of a tower, an arm in armour embowed, all ppr., grasping a pennon of St George; a leopard's head guardant, erased at the neck, or
Thorpe	a cock gu., beaked, combed, legged and wattled or
Tindall	out of a ducal coronet or, a plume of feathers erm., within a basket gu.
Todd	a wolf's head, or, collared flory counterflory, gu.; a fox sejant, ppr.
Trotter	a horse trotting, ar.; a galley, with oars in action
Tucker	a lion's gamb erect and erased, gu., charged with three billets fesswise, or, in the foot a battle-axe, ar., handle of the second.
Turner	a lion passant, gu., in its dexter paw a laurel branch, vert; on a tower ar., with broken battlements, an eagle regardant, sa.; a flaming heart ppr.
Underwood	a lion's gamb holding a thistle, ppr.
Upton	on a chapeau az., turned up erm., a griffin passant, ar.
Urquhart	a boar's head couped, gu.
Usher	a Doric pillar ar., winged or
Vaughan	on a plume of three feathers, gu., a griffin's head or; a boy's head, couped at the shoulders, ppr., with snakes entwined about his neck, vert

Vernon	a demi-female, habited vert, holding under her sinister arm a garb or, in her dexter hand a sickle of the last, headed ppr.
Wade	a boar salient, sa., collared or
Walker	a swan swimming in a loch, ppr.; a lion in a wood, all ppr.; a demi-heraldic tiger, per pale indented ar. and sa., armed, langued and tuskedgu., mane and tail purfled, or; a rock ppr.
Wall	a demi-lion rampant guardant, az., holding a battle-axe, headed ar., handled gu.
Walsh	a cubit arm, in the hand a tilting spear, ppr.
Walton	a dragon's head couped, or, flames issuing from the mouth, ppr., on the neck a cross pattée, sa.
Ward	out of a mural coronet or, a wolf's head, per fess, or and az.; a dove and olive branch, ppr.; a buck passant, ppr., collared, lined and ringed, gold
Warner	a horse's head erased, per fess erm. and gu., maned of the last
Warren	on a chapeau gu., turned up erm., a wyvern ar., wings chequy or and az.; a dragon's head gu.
Watkins	a dragon's head erased, vert, in the mouth a dexter hand couped at the wrist, gu.
Watson	on a mount vert, a palm tree or; two arms issuing from clouds, holding the stump of a tree, fructed at the top, with branches on each side, all ppr.
Watt	a falcon ppr., hooded and belled, or
Watts	a greyhound sejant, ar., supporting with the dexter paw an arrow or, headed and barbed of the first; a griffin's head erased, in the beak an annulet
Webb	a hind's head erased, ppr., vulned in the neck, gu.
Webster	the sun rising from the sea, ppr.
Weir	a demi-horse in armour, ppr., bridled and saddled, gu.
Wells	a fire beacon ppr.; a demi-lion rampant
West	a griffin's head erased, per pale wavy or and az.; a demi-dragon ppr., without tail, collared or, in the dexter claw a sword, also ppr.
Wheeler	a camel's head erased, vert, bezantée; a rose branch, ppr., flowered gu.
White	a lion's head erased, or, collared vairé, gold and vert; an ermine, ppr.; an ostrich ar.

Wilkins	a demi-griffin regardant, gu., in the dexter claw a sword in pale, ar., hilt and pommel or
Wilkinson	out of a mural coronet gu., a demi-unicorn rampant, erminois, erased of the first, armed and maned or; a fire beacon inflamed, ppr.; on a mount vert, a greyhound sejant, ar., gorged with a collar, sa., rimmed and ringed or, on the dexter part of the mount a laurel branch of the first
Williams	a bustard close; a cock gu., combed and legged or; a tower ar., and out of its battlements an arm embowed in mail, in the hand, ppr., a broken lance, point downwards and guttée de sang
Williamson	out of a mural coronet, a dragon's head vomiting flames
Willis	a hind trippant, ppr., in its mouth an oak branch ar., fructed or, on the shoulder a cross formée of the last
Wilson	a talbot's head erased, az., on the neck three ingots of gold in fess, crossed by another in bend, ppr.; a wolf salient, or; a lion's gamb erect and erased
Winchester	a hand holding a cluster of grapes, ppr.
Winter	a hind passant, ar.; a hawk ar., in its dexter claw a fish erect, or
Wiseman	a tower or, port ar., on the top a demi-moor (vested in mail), all ppr., wreathed round the temples, ar. and sa., in the dexter hand a dart of the first, plumed and headed of the second, in the sinister a Roman shield of the first
Wood	a ship in full sail ppr.; an oak tree fructed, ppr.; an oak tree ppr., charged with acorns, or; a woodman, holding in his dexter hand an oak slip, in his sinister a club, resting upon his shoulders, all ppr.
Woodward	a demi-lion rampant, sa., supporting between its paws a pheon or
Wright	a dragon's head erased, ar., pellettée; a wheatsheaf or, environed by an antique crown sa.; a dexter arm holding a battle-axe, ppr.
Wyatt	an ostrich gu., the tail bezantée, in its beak a horseshoe sa.
York	a thistle ppr.
Young	an ibex ar., attired or, issuing from a ducal coronet or; a lion rampant guardant, per fess or and gu., supporting a battle-axe, gold

GLOSSARY

This glossary provides a quick source of reference to over two hundred terms used in heraldry. It does not aim to be exhaustive but does encompass the commonest terms and concepts. In most cases the text will provide greater detail, and often these definitions will be exemplified by an illustration.

abatement a mark of dishonour, the opposite of AUGMENTATION.

achievement the complete coat of arms, comprising crest, helmet, mantling, motto, fully emblazoned.

addorsed *or* **endorsed** a term meaning 'set back to back', usually applied to animals and wings.

affronté when an animal is depicted facing forwards to show the full face.

angled a line of partition that consists of a straight line with a vertical step in the middle.

annulet one of the subordinaries, comprising a small circular ring.

apaumé when used as a charge and the hand is shown open with the palm visible.

arched a line of partition, little used but comprising a long arc.

arg. the abbreviation for ARGENT.

argent the heraldic term for the METAL silver. The abbreviation is **arg**.

armed the term used when the beak, teeth, horns, talons or hoofs of the appropriate animal are depicted in a different tincture from the body.

armigerous having the right to bear arms.

augmentation a special mark of honour given by the sovereign in recognition of some action.

az. the abbreviation for AZURE (blue).

azure the heraldic term for the COLOUR blue. The abbreviation, used in BLAZONING, is **az**.

badge an indication of ownership in ancient times. Now a type of emblem that does not form part of the ACHIEVEMENT.

banner a type of flag and the main flag of a knight. It carried the arms as found on the shield.

bar one of the ORDINARIES, similar to the FESS but not as wide.

barrulé an alternative for the term BARRULY.

barrulet a diminutive, smaller version of the BAR.

barruly the term applied when the divisions of a field BARRY exceed eight in number.

barry a term used to describe a field that is divided horizontally into an even number of equal parts, six or eight.

barry nebuly a field BARRY divided with the partition line NEBULY.

bars gemelles a pair of thin BARRULETS.

beaked when the beak of a bird is shown in a TINCTURE different from the rest of the body.

belled signifying a falcon or hawk that is shown with a bell on one or both legs.

bend one of the ORDINARIES, which consists of a diagonal band across the field. It runs from dexter chief to sinister base on the shield (top left to bottom right when looking at the shield).

bendlet the diminutive, smaller version of the BEND, which is about half the width of the bend.

bend sinister a bend running sinister chief to dexter base, opposite to the BEND.

bendy the term to describe a field divided into several BENDS diagonally.

bezant *or* **besant** a representation of a gold coin of Byzantium. It appears as a gold disc but the colour is not stated, it is always gold.

billet one of the SUBORDINARIES, which resembles a rectangular block.

billetté a field that is SEMÉ of BILLETS.

blazon the process by which all the details of a coat of arms are described using the proper heraldic terminology.

blazoning the written description of the arrangement of charges, etc, on a shield. *Compare* EMBLAZONING.

bordure a border around the edge of a shield that may have different lines of partition applied to the inner edge.

bouget an old term for a water bucket, which features as a charge on shields, although its heraldic representation is somewhat removed from the actuality.

caboshed the term for the head of a beast shown facing forward, without any part of the neck.

cadency the means whereby brothers of the same family and families of brothers are distinguished in heraldry using marks of DIFFERENCE.

canton a small QUARTER, and DIMINUTIVE of it, that is commonly placed in the DEXTER CHIEF of a shield. It is used as a mark of DIFFERENCE or AUGMENTATION.

cap of maintenance *see* CHAPEAU.

chapeau *or* **cap of maintenance** *or* **cap of dignity**, a scarlet velvet hat lined with ermine, with the edge turned up and split at the back.

charge any figure or device that features upon a shield.

chequy *or* **chequé** when the field or an ORDINARY is shown with alternate squares of METAL or COLOUR and FUR.

chevron an ORDINARY consisting of an inverted V shape, with the two legs touching the DEXTER and SINISTER base points of the field.

chevronel the diminutive form of the CHEVRON.

chevronny a field that is full of CHEVRONS, producing parallel lines in the shape of the V over the whole field.

chief one of the ORDINARIES, which comprises a rectangular broad band filling the upper third of the shield but which in practice is often less.

cinquefoil a five-leaved flower type of CHARGE, similar in origin to the TREFOIL.

colour one of three types of TINCTURE in heraldry, the others being METAL and FUR. The major colours are gules (red), sable (black), azure (blue), vert (green) and purpure (purple).

combatant the term when two heraldic animals are RAMPANT, facing each other.

comble a Scottish DIMINUTIVE of the CHIEF.

compony *or* **gobony** the term for a BORDURE, BEND, PALE or other ORDINARY that has alternate squares of METAL and COLOUR.

conjoined the heraldic term for two elements that are joined together.

contrevair *or* COUNTER VAIR a variation of the fur VAIR in which the points and bases of the shield-like shapes of one row meet those of the rows above and below (*see* figure 5).

cotise a DIMINUTIVE of the BEND, which is about one quarter of the width of the bend and half the width of a BENDLET.

couché is when a shield is drawn in a diagonal position.

counter compony two rows of alternate squares of METAL and COLOUR.

counter flory FLEURS-DE-LIS that are placed alternately in contrary directions.

counter potent a variation of the fur, POTENT.

counter vair *see* CONTREVAIR.

couped the term for when an ORDINARY is cut short of the sides of the shield. Also, when the head or other parts of animals are cut off to be used as a charge, a clean cut is called couped.

courant the term used to describe a stag when it is running.

coward *see* COWED.

cowed *or* **coward** the term for when an animal is depicted with its tail between its legs.

crest the ornament on the top of the helmet.

crined when the hair upon a charge, usually that of a human figure, is depicted in a different TINCTURE from that of the body.

cross an ORDINARY shaped as a cross, essentially made up of a PALE and a FESS joining at their midpoints. There are many varieties of cross.

cross-crosslet a CROSS with a further cross on each arm.

crusily a field scattered with CROSS CROSSLETS (or other types of cross).

dancetté a line of PARTITION consisting of a serrated edge that is usually drawn with three complete 'teeth'.

debruised the term used when a charge has an ORDINARY placed over it. The charge is debruised.

dexter the left side of the shield when viewed from the front.

difference the name for an element that is used in a coat of arms to differentiate between branches of a family.

dimidiation in the MARSHALLING of arms, an old and no longer used method of conjoining the arms of a husband and wife by merging half of each shield into one.

diminutive a subsidiary version of an ORDINARY, which is usually thinner and/or smaller, e.g. the BENDLET is the diminutive of the BEND.

disarmed the term for an heraldic lion when it is depicted without claws, teeth or tongue.

double-queued refers to the lion RAMPANT when it is shown with two tails, each emanating from the base.

dovetailed a line of PARTITION comprising dovetails, i.e. made up of reversed wedges.

embattled a line of PARTITION that has a shape similar to the outline of the battlements of a tower.

emblazoning the craft of painting a coat of arms with all its ORDINARIES and charges. *Compare* BLAZONING.

embowed the term for an arm (shoulder to fingertips) that is bent at the elbow.

endorsed *see* ADDORSED.

engrailed a line of PARTITION that has a series of semicircles joined to form cusps with the points turned outwards. It is a style often used on ORDINARIES.

enhanced a term used to refer to BENDLETS when they are placed higher towards the CHIEF than normal.

erased a term for when the head or limb of an animal, used as a charge, shows a jagged edge.

eradicated a term used when the roots of a tree are shown on an ACHIEVEMENT.

ermine one of the two basic FURS, comprising white fur with black marks or spots.

ermines a variation of the ERMINE fur, comprising white spots on a black ground.

erminois a variation of the ERMINE fur, comprising black spots on a gold background.

escutcheon the technical term for the shield in heraldry. Also, the term used to describe an INESCUTCHEON placed other than in the centre of a field.

estoile *or* **etoile** a charge that is like a star but with wavy rays.

fess a band that runs horizontally across the shield and occupies the middle third so that the fess point is in the middle of the band.

field the surface of the shield upon which the heraldic design is placed.

fillet the diminutive form of the CHIEF.

fimbriated a term used when an ORDINARY is shown with a narrow border of a different TINCTURE.

fitched *or* **fitchée** a term used when a cross has the bottom part pointed.

flanches *or* **flaunches** two curved lines, one on either side of the field, which always occur in pairs.

fleur-de-lis the heraldic lily, which has its origins in the arms of France.

flory decorated with FLEURS-DE-LIS.

fountain a type of ROUNDEL that consists of a varied field, barry wavy, argent and azure.

fret a SUBORDINARY that is made up of a voided LOZENGE that is interwoven with two BENDLETS or RIBANDS in SALTIRE.

fretty a field covered with a network of RIBANDS and ribands SINISTER interlacing with each other in alternate fashion.

fructed the term meaning bearing fruit or seeds.

furs one of the TINCTURES used in colouring shields. The two basic furs are ERMINE and VAIR.

fusil a SUBORDINARY that is a variation of the LOZENGE but is narrower and longer.

gamb a word derived from Old French that is used for the leg of a lion or other animal.

garb the term used to describe any sheaf (of grain, etc) in heraldry.

garter one of the identifying insignia of the most noble order of the Knights of the Garter. It is made of blue velvet edged with gold and bears their motto. Also a very rarely encountered diminutive of the BEND, which in width is between that of the BENDLET and COTISE.

gemelle a term signifying double, usually found in BARS GE-MELLES.

gobony an alternative term for COMPONY.

gorged a term used when an animal of any description is shown with a collar round the neck. A common example is 'ducally gorged', when the collar is a coronet.

gu. the abbreviation for GULES (red).

guardant a term used when an animal is shown with the head facing fully forward.

guidon a type of flag, found in Scottish heraldry, that is slightly smaller than the STANDARD.

gules the heraldic term for the COLOUR red. The abbreviation, used in BLAZONING, is **gu.**

guttée *or* **gutté** a field sprinkled (or SEMÉE) with drops. These may be silver, gold, de sang (blood), de larmes (tears), de poix (black), etc.

gyron a triangular SUBORDINARY that is formed by two lines from the centre of the shield to its edge.

gyronny a division of the field into GYRONS.

hatching the monochrome representation of the various TINCTURES used in heraldry.

hauriant the description when a fish is shown vertically on a shield, with the head pointing upwards.

imbrued the term used to describe a weapon that has spots of blood upon it.

impaled the term for two coats of arms conjoined in one shield palewise.

indented a line of PARTITION that has a serrated edge, and may consist of any number of points.

inescutcheon a shield forming a charge on another shield, placed in the centre of the field. If placed elsewhere it is simply called an escutcheon.

invected a line of PARTITION that in effect is the opposite of ENGRAILED. It has a series of semicircles joined to form cusps with the points turned inwards. It is a style often used on ORDINARIES.

jessed a term used when a bell on the leg of a falcon is attached by a leather strap, the jess.

joust an event at a TOURNAMENT in which knights fought a duel.

label a mark of DIFFERENCE in CADENCY that indicates the eldest son in a family.

lambrequin an alternative term for the MANTLING.

langued the term used when the tongue of an animal is shown in a TINCTURE different from that used for the rest of the body.

lines of partition *see* PARTITION.

livery colours the principal METAL and COLOUR from the shield.

lodged a term used with reference to a stag when it is sitting with the head erect.

lozenge a diamond-shaped charge and SUBORDINARY. Also, the shield shape upon which the arms of a lady or widow are displayed.

manche *see* MAUNCHE.

mantling *or* **lambrequin** the veil-like cloth that is draped from the top of the helmet, down either side of the shield.

marshalling the practice that shows on one shield the joining together of two or more coats of arms because of marriage, alliance or descent, and over several generations.

mascle a LOZENGE that is voided, which therefore has a lozenge-shaped hole in the centre.

maunche *or* **manche** an old-fashioned sleeve used as a charge.

membered a term used when the legs of a bird are shown in a colour different from that of the body.

metal one of the TINCTURES used in heraldry. There are two metals, gold and silver, which are called or and argent respectively. One metal cannot be placed upon another except for special reasons.

motto a word or brief sentence associated with the crest. It is often placed inside a scroll and then beneath the shield (in England) or above the crest (in Scotland). It often links with the name of the bearer and charges on the shield.

mullet a five-pointed star that occurs as a charge.

mural a term applied to a coronet or crown when it is depicted as being made of stone, as if it were a castle wall. The rim is bedecked with towers.

naiant the term used to describe a fish placed horizontally on the shield.

nebuly a curvy line of PARTITION that has its origin attributed to the shape of clouds.

nowed a term used to describe the intertwining and interlacing form shown by a serpent.

ogress a black ROUNDEL.

ondé *see* WAVY.

ordinaries a group of charges, each of which comprises a simple shape. They were used at the outset of heraldry and include the BEND, BAR, PALE, CHIEF, FESS, PILE, CROSS, SALTIRE and CHEVRON.

orle a BORDURE that occurs within the shield forming a narrow band following the shape of the shield and set in from the edge at roughly the depth of a bordure.

pairle an ORDINARY in the shape of a letter Y, which is also known as the pall or the shakefork.

pale one of the ORDINARIES, which comprises a band running vertically down the centre of the field from chief to base. It is meant to occupy one third of the field.

pall *see* PAIRLE.

pallet the diminutive form of the PALE, which is about half the width.

paly the term for when the field is divided by vertical lines, i.e. is made up of an equal number of PALES.

parted the Scottish term for PARTY.

partition the means by which fields are divided. The lines of partition occur in a number different styles. The main lines of partition are DANCETTÉ, DOVETAILED, EMBATTLED, ENGRAILED, INDENTED, INVECTED, NEBULY, POTENTÉ and RAGULY.

party a term used to describe a shield that is divided by a line that follows the line of one of the ORDINARIES.

passant the position of an heraldic animal when it is shown with one foot raised, a position in which it is considered to be walking.

pean the name of one of the ERMINE furs that has gold spots on a black background.

pellet a black ROUNDEL.

pennon a small type of flag that was essentially triangular in shape and was carried on a lance.

pile a triangular wedge-like ORDINARY projecting downwards from the top of the field.

pinsel a small triangular flag found in Scottish heraldry.

plate a silver ROUNDEL.

potent one of the FURS, which resembles a simple crutch in outline.

potenté a line of PARTITION resembling the outline of the POTENT fur.

proper a term used when describing a charge on a shield to indicate that the item is represented in its natural colours.

purfle an ornamental border.

purp. the abbreviation for PURPURE (purple).

purpure the heraldic term for the COLOUR purple. The abbreviation, used in BLAZONING, is **purp**.

quarter literally one quarter of a field that has been divided quarterly.

quartering the division of the shield into quarters, and possible subdivision of the quarters thus formed. Also a method of MARSHALLING arms in which the arms of husband and wife are combined in opposite quarters.

quarterings quarters that have arms charged upon them.

quatrefoil a four-leaved flower type of charge, similar in origin to the TREFOIL.

queue-fourché the term for a forked tail on the heraldic lion.

raguly a line of partition consisting of sloping crenellations.

rampant the term used to describe the position of an heraldic animal when it is shown rearing up on its hind legs with one paw or claw raised.

rayonné a line of partition that resembles triangular but flickering tongues of flame.

regardant the term used to describe an animal that is is looking back over its shoulder.

riband a diminutive of the bend, which is half the width of the cotise.

rising the term used to describe a bird that is about to take off.

roundel the collective name for charges of small circles, e.g. bezant, torteau and pellet.

rustre a lozenge with a circular hole at the centre.

sa. the abbreviation for SABLE (black).

sable the heraldic term for the COLOUR black. The abbreviation, used in BLAZONING, is **sa**.

sachsen the bones of the wings, particularly as seen in the heraldic eagle.

salient the term used to describe a springing stag with both hind feet on the ground.

saltire a diagonal cross made up of a BEND and a bend SINISTER meeting at their midpoints. It is also known as the Cross of St Andrew.

scarp a diminutive form of the BEND sinister.

segreant the term applied by some authorities to a GRIFFIN in the RAMPANT position.

sejant the term used to describe an animal that is sitting.

semé the French word for 'strewed' or 'strewn'. When a field is scattered with an object, it is semé.

shakefork *see* PAIRLE.

sinister the right side of the shield when viewed fom the front.

slipped the term used to describe a TREFOIL with its stalk.

standard a long, narrow and highly ornamented flag that commonly carried the owner's badge, certain charges and the cross of St George (or the relevant saint).

statant the term used to describe the position of an heraldic animal when it is shown standing with all four paws on the ground and facing to the right (i.e. dexter).

subordinaries a subordinate group of ORDINARIES that occur less frequently than the ordinaries.

superimposition a method of marshalling arms in which the arms of a wife are placed on top of her husband's by means of an INESCUTCHEON of pretence.

supporters animals, birds, beasts or human figures that are placed on either side of a shield in an ACHIEVEMENT and look as if they are holding up the shield.

tincture the heraldic term for COLOUR. Tinctures are divided into colours, metals and furs.

torse another term for the WREATH.

tournament a public exhibition of combat in which knights fought for reputation and honour.

tourney *or* **meleé** something of a free-for-all combat at a tournament event undertaken by teams who usually used wooden weapons.

trefoil a charge comprising three 'leaves', similar to the shamrock.

trellis a variation of FRETTY, in which the BENDLETS OR RIBANDS are not interwoven, but the bendlets lie upon the bendlets sinister, and they are nailed at the intersections.

tressure a SUBORDINARY made up of two ORLES, one inside the other (an orle gemelle), which is placed quite near to the edge of the ESCUTCHEON.

trippant the term used to describe a stag that is shown walking.

undy *see* WAVY.

unguled the term for when the nails, claws, hooves, talons of a breast are shown in a TINCTURE different from that of the principal charge. Also used specifically for the hoof of an animal.

vair one of the heraldic FURS, which is meant to represent squirrel and consists of rows of alternating blue and white cup shapes (azure and argent).

vair en pointe a variation of the VAIR fur.

vair in pale a variation of the VAIR fur producing a columnar arrangement.

vert the heraldic term for the COLOUR green. It has no abbreviation and is used in full in BLAZONING.

visitation the process whereby heralds travelled the country to check upon all claims to bear a coat of arms.

volant the term applied to a bird that is flying.

vulned the term meaning 'wounded' when applied to an animal.

wavy *or* **undy** *or* **ondé** a curved PARTITION line that probably had its origin in the waves seen in water.

wreath a circular configuration of two strands twisted together, resembling a rope. It is placed around the dome of the helmet and at the base of the crest.

APPENDIX

ORDER OF PRECEDENCE

The Sovereign

The Prince of Wales

Younger sons of the Sovereign

Grandsons of the Sovereign

Brothers of the Sovereign

Uncles of the Sovereign

The Sovereign's brothers' or sisters' sons (according to the seniority of their parents)

The Archbishop of Canterbury, Lord Primate of All England

The Lord High Chancellor, or Lord Keeper

The Archbishop of York, Primate of England

The Prime Minister

The Lord Chancellor of Ireland

The Lord High Treasurer

The Lord President of the Privy Council

The Speaker of the House of Commons

The Lord Privy Seal

The Lord Great Chamberlain

The Lord High Constable	⎤ Above
The Earl Marshal	peers of
The Lord High Admiral	their
The Lord Steward of His or Her Majesty's Household	own
The Lord Chamberlain of His or Her Majesty's Household	⎦ degree

The Master of Horse

Dukes, according to their patents of creation, England, Scotland, Great Britain, Ireland, United Kingdom, and of Ireland since 1801

Eldest sons of dukes of the royal blood

Marquesses, according to their patents of creation, England, Scotland, Great Britain, Ireland, United Kingdom, and of Ireland since the Union

Dukes' eldest sons

177

Earls, according to their patents as aforesaid

Younger sons of dukes of Royal blood

Marquesses' eldest sons

Dukes' younger sons

Viscounts, according to their patents as aforesaid

Earls' eldest sons

Marquesses' younger sons

Bishops of London, Durham and Winchester

All other English bishops, according to their seniority of consecration

Secretaries of State and Chief Secretary to Lord Lieutenant of
  Ireland, if of the degree of a baron

Barons, according to their patents as aforesaid

Lords of Appeal in Ordinary

Commissioner of the Great Seal

Treasurer of His or Her Majesty's Household

Comptroller of His or Her Majesty's Household

Vice-Chamberlain of His or Her Majesty's Household

Secretaries of State and Chief Secretary to Lord Lieutenant of Ireland
  under the degree of barons

Viscounts' eldest sons

Earls' younger sons

Barons' eldest sons

Knights of the Most Noble Order of The Garter

Knights of St Patrick

Privy Councillors

Chancellor of the Exchequer

Chancellor of the Duchy of Lancaster

Lord Chief Justice of England

Master of the Rolls

The Lords Justices of the Court of Appeal, and President of the
  Probate, Divorce and Admiralty Divisions, according to seniority
  and order of appointment

Judges of the High Court of Justice rank among themselves according
  to date of appointment

Viscounts' younger sons

Barons' younger sons

Sons of Lords of Appeal in Ordinary (life peers), according to
  seniority of creation

Baronets of England, Scotland, and Ireland
Knights Grand Cross of the Bath
Knights Grand Commanders of the Star of India
Knights Grand Cross of St Michael and St George
Knights Grand Commanders of the Order of the Indian Empire
Knights Grand Cross of the Royal Victorian Order
Knights Grand Cross of the Order of the British Empire
Knights Commanders of the Bath
Knights Commanders of the Star of India
Knights Commanders of St Michael and St George
Knights Commanders of the Order of the Indian Empire
Knights Commanders of the Royal Victorian Order
Knights Commanders of the Order of the British Empire
Knights Bachelors
Judges of County Courts in England and Wales and of City of London
    Court
Serjeants at Law
Masters in Lunacy
Companions of the Bath
Companions of the Star of India
Companions of St Michael and St George
Companions of the Indian Empire
Commanders of the Royal Victorian Order
Commanders of the Order of the British Empire
Companions of the Distinguished Service Order
Members of the 4th class of the Royal Victorian Order
Officers of the Order of the British Empire
Companions of the Imperial Service Order
Eldest sons of the younger sons of peers
Baronets' eldest sons
Eldest sons of Knights of the Garter
Eldest sons of Knights Bachelors
Members of the 5th class of the Royal Victorian Order
Members of the Order of the British Empire
Baronets' younger sons
Younger sons of knights
Esquires
Gentlemen

ORDER OF PRECEDENCE AMONG WOMEN IN ENGLAND
The Queen
The Queen Dowager
The Princess of Wales

Princesses, daughters of the Sovereign
Princesses and duchesses, wives of the Sovereign's sons
Granddaughters of the Sovereign
Wives of the Sovereign's grandsons
The Sovereign's sisters
Wives of the Sovereign's brothers
The Sovereign's aunts
Wives of the Sovereign's uncles
Daughters of dukes of the Royal blood
Wives of the Sovereign's nephews
Granddaughters of Sovereign not bearing style of Royal Highness
Duchesses of England, Scotland, Great Britain, Ireland and United
   Kingdom
Wives of the eldest sons of dukes of the Royal blood
Marchionesses of England, Scotland, Great Britain, Ireland and
   United Kingdom
Wives of the eldest sons of dukes
Daughters of dukes
Countesses of England, Scotland, Great Britain, Ireland and United
   Kingdom
Wives of younger sons of dukes of Royal blood
Wives of the eldest sons of marquesses
Daughters of marquesses
Wives of the younger sons of dukes
Viscountesses of England, Scotland, Great Britain, Ireland and United
   Kingdom
Wives of the eldest sons of earls
Daughters of earls
Wives of the younger sons of marquesses
Baronesses of England, Scotland, Great Britain, Ireland and United
   Kingdom
Wives of Lords of Appeal in Ordinary (life peers), according to
   seniority of creation of title
Wives of the eldest sons of viscounts

Daughters of viscounts
Wives of the younger sons of earls
Wives of the eldest sons of barons
Dame Commanders of the Order of the British Empire
Daughters of barons
Maids of Honour
Wives of Knights of the Garter
Wives of Knights of St Patrick
Wives of the younger sons of viscounts
Wives of the younger sons of barons
Daughters of Lords of Appeal in Ordinary (life peers)
Wives of sons of Lords of Appeal in Ordinary (life peers)
Wives of baronets
Wives of Knights Grand Cross of the Order of the Bath
Wives of Knights Grand Commanders of the Star of India
Wives of Knights Grand Cross of St Michael and St George
Wives of Knights Grand Commanders of the Order of the Indian
    Empire
Wives of Knights Grand Cross of the Royal Victorian Order
Wives of Knights Grand Cross of the Order of the British Empire
Wives of Knights Commanders of the Order of the Bath
Wives of Knights Commanders of the Star of India
Wives of Knights Commanders of St Michael and St George
Wives of Knights Commanders of the Indian Empire
Wives of Knights Commanders of the Royal Victorian Order
Wives of Knights Commanders of the Order of the British Empire
Wives of Knights Bachelors
Commanders of the Order of the British Empire
Wives of Companions of the Bath
Wives of Companions of the Star of India
Wives of Companions of St Michael and St George
Wives of Companions of the Indian Empire
Wives of Commanders of the Royal Victorian Order
Wives of Commanders of the Order of the British Empire
Wives of Companions of the Distinguished Service Order
Officers of the Order of the British Empire
Wives of members of the 4th class of the Royal Victorian Order
Wives of officers of the Order of the British Empire

Companions of the Imperial Service Order
Wives of Companions of the Imperial Service Order
Wives of the eldest sons of the younger sons of peers
Daughters of the younger sons of peers
Wives of the eldest sons of baronets
Daughters of baronets
Wives of the eldest sons of Knights of the Garter
Wives of the eldest sons of Knights Bachelors
Daughters of Knights Bachelors
Members of the Order of the British Empire
Wives of members of the 5th class of the Royal Victorian Order
Wives of members of the Order of the British Empire
Wives of members of the Imperial Service Order
Wives of the younger sons of the younger sons of peers
Wives of the younger sons of baronets
Wives of the younger sons of knights
Wives of esquires
Wives of gentlemen

ORDER OF PRECEDENCE AMONG MEN IN SCOTLAND
The Sovereign

The Lord High Commissioner to the General Assembly of the Church
    of Scotland during the sitting of the General Assembly
Duke of Rothesay
Younger sons of the Sovereign
Grandsons of the Sovereign
Brothers of the Sovereign
Uncles of the Sovereign
Nephews of the Sovereign
Note
    Lords Lieutenant of counties
    Lord Provosts of cities being *ex officio* Lords Lieutenant of
    counties of cities
    Sheriffs Principal during their term of office, and within the
    bounds of their respective counties, cities, and sheriffdoms, shall
    have precedence next after the Royal Family and the Lord High
    Commissioner
    Every Lord Lieutenant of a county and every Lord Lieutenant of

a county of a city during his term of office, and within the limits of his jurisdiction, shall have precedence before the Sheriff Principal having concurrent jurisdiction in the said county or county of a city

The Lord Chancellor of Great Britain

The Moderator of the General Assembly of the Church of Scotland during his term of office

The Prime Minister

The Keeper of the Great Seal of Scotland (the Secretary for Scotland) (if a peer)

The Speaker of the House of Commons

The Keeper of the Privy Seal of Scotland (if a peer)

The Hereditary High Constable of Scotland

The Hereditary Master of the Household in Scotland

Dukes of England

Dukes of Scotland

Dukes of Great Britain

Dukes of United Kingdom and dukes of Ireland created since 1801

Eldest sons of dukes of royal blood

Marquesses of England

Marquesses of Scotland

Marquesses of Great Britain

Marquesses of the United Kingdom and marquesses of Ireland created since the union of Great Britain and Ireland

Eldest sons of dukes

Earls of England

Earls of Scotland

Earls of Great Britain

Earls of United Kingdom and Earls of Ireland created since 1801

Younger sons of dukes of Royal blood

Eldest sons of marquesses

Younger sons of dukes

The Keeper of the Great Seal (the Secretary for Scotland) (if not a peer)

The Keeper of the Privy Seal (if not a peer)

The Lord Justice General

The Lord Clerk Register

The Lord Advocate

The Lord Justice Clerk
Viscounts of England
Viscounts of Scotland
Viscounts of Great Britain
Viscounts of the United Kingdom and Viscounts of Ireland created
  since the union of Great Britain and Ireland
Eldest sons of earls
Younger sons of marquesses
Barons of England
Barons of Scotland
Barons of Great Britain
Barons of United Kingdom and Barons of Ireland created since 1801
Eldest sons of viscounts
Younger sons of earls
Eldest sons of barons
Knights of the Garter
Privy Councillors
Senators of the College of Justice and Chairman of the Land Court
Younger sons of viscounts
Younger sons of barons
Sons of law life peers
Baronets
Knights of the Thistle
Knights of St Patrick
Knights Grand Cross of the Order of the Bath
Knights Grand Commanders of the Order of the Star of India
Knights Grand Cross of the Order of St Michael and St George
Knights Grand Commanders of the Order of the Indian Empire
Knights Grand Cross of the Royal Victorian Order
Knights Grand Cross of the Order of the British Empire
Knights Commanders of the Order of the Bath
Knights Commanders of the Order of the Star of India
Knights Commanders of the Order of St Michael and St George
Knights Commanders of the Order of the Indian Empire
Knights Commanders of the Royal Victorian Order
Knights Commanders of the Order of the British Empire
Solicitor General for Scotland
Lyon King of Arms

Sheriffs Principal
Knights Bachelor
Sheriffs Substitute
Companions of the Order of the Bath
Companions of the Order of the Star of India
Companions of the Order of St Michael and St George
Companions of the Order of the Indian Empire
Commanders of the Royal Victorian Order
Commanders of the Order of the British Empire
Companions of the Distinguished Service Order
Members of the 4th class of the Royal Victorian Order
Officers of the Order of the British Empire
Imperial Service Order
Eldest sons of younger sons of peers
Eldest sons of baronets
Eldest sons of knights
Members of the 5th class of the Royal Victorian Order
Members of the Order of the British Empire
Younger sons of baronets
Younger sons of knights
King's Counsel
Esquires
Gentlemen

ORDER OF PRECEDENCE AMONG WOMEN IN SCOTLAND
The Queen
The Queen Dowager

Duchess of Rothesay
Daughters of the Sovereign
Wives of younger sons of the Sovereign
Granddaughters of the Sovereign
Wives of grandsons of the Sovereign
Sisters of the Sovereign
Wives of brothers of the Sovereign
Aunts of the Sovereign
Wives of uncles of the Sovereign
Nieces of the Sovereign

Wives of nephews of the Sovereign

Duchesses in the rank of their husbands, namely

—duchesses of England

—duchesses of Scotland

—duchesses of Great Britain

—duchesses of the United Kingdom and duchesses of Ireland of titles created since the union of Great Britain and Ireland.

Wives of the eldest sons of dukes of royal blood

Marchionesses in the rank of their husbands, namely

—marchionesses of England

—marchionesses of Scotland

—marchionesses of Great Britain

—marchionesses of the United Kingdom and marchionesses of Ireland of titles created since the union of Great Britain and Ireland

Wives of eldest sons of dukes

Daughters of dukes

Countesses in the rank of their husbands, namely

—countesses of England

—countesses of Scotland

—countesses of Great Britain

—countesses of the United Kingdom and countesses of Ireland of titles created since the union of Great Britain and Ireland

Wives of younger sons of dukes of Royal blood

Wives of eldest sons of marquesses

Daughters of marquesses

Wives of younger sons of dukes

Viscountesses in the rank of their husbands, namely

—viscountesses of England

—viscountesses of Scotland

—viscountesses of Great Britain

—viscountesses of the United Kingdom and viscountesses of Ireland of titles created since 1801

Wives of eldest sons of earls

Daughters of earls

Wives of younger sons of marquesses

Baronesses in the rank of their husbands, namely

—baronesses of England

—baronesses of Scotland

—baronesses of Great Britain

—baronesses of the United Kingdom and baronesses of Ireland of titles created since the union of Great Britain and Ireland

Wives of eldest sons of viscounts

Daughters of viscounts

Wives of younger sons of earls

Wives of eldest sons of barons

Daughters of barons

Maids of Honour to the Queen

Wives of Knights of the Garter

Wives of younger sons of viscounts

Wives of younger sons of barons

Daughters of law life peers (Lords of Appeal in Ordinary)

Wives of sons of law life peers (Lords of Appeal in Ordinary)

Wives of baronets

Wives of Knights of the Thistle

Wives of Knights of St Patrick

Dames Grand Cross of the Order of the British Empire

Wives of Knights Grand Cross of the Order of the Bath

Wives of Knights Grand Commanders of the Order of the Star of India

Wives of Knights Grand Cross of the Order of St Michael and St George

Wives of Knights Grand Commanders of the Order of the Indian Empire

Wives of Knights Grand Cross of the Royal Victorian Order

Wives of Knights Grand Cross of the Order of the British Empire

Dame Commanders of the Order of the British Empire

Wives of Knights Commanders of the Order of the Bath

Wives of Knights Commanders of the Order of the Star of India

Wives of Knights Commanders of the Order of St Michael and St George

Wives of Knights Commanders of the Order of the Indian Empire

Wives of Knights Commanders of the Royal Victorian Order

Wives of Knights Commanders of the Order of the British Empire

Wives of Knights Bachelor and wives of senators of the College of Justice (Lords of Session), and of the chairman of the Land Court. Taking precedence among themselves according to the dates of

their husbands' creation as knights or appointment as senators of
the College of Justice respectively
Commanders of the Order of the British Empire
Wives of Companions of the Order of the Bath
Wives of Companions of the Order of the Star of India
Wives of Companions of the Order of St Michael and St George
Wives of Companions of the Order of the Indian Empire
Wives of Commanders of the Royal Victorian Order
Wives of Commanders of the Order of the British Empire
Wives of Companions of the Distinguished Service Order
Officers of the Order of the British Empire
Wives of members of the 4th class of the Royal Victorian Order
Wives of eldest sons of younger sons of peers
Daughters of younger sons of peers
Wives of eldest sons of baronets
Daughters of baronets
Wives of eldest sons of Knights of the Garter, of the Thistle, and of St
Patrick
Wives of eldest sons of knights
Daughters of knights
Members of the Order of the British Empire
Wives of members of the 4th class of the Royal Victorian Order
Wives of members of the Order of the British Empire
Members of Imperial Service Order
Wives of members of the Imperial Service Order
Wives of younger sons of baronets
Wives of younger sons of knights
Wives of esquires
Wives of gentlemen.